ENGLISH CASTLES

A PHOTOGRAPHIC HISTORY

ENGLISH CASTLES
A PHOTOGRAPHIC HISTORY

by Rodney Castleden

Quercus

Quercus Publishing
46 Dorset Street
London
W1U 7NB

First published 2006

A catalogue record for this book is available from the British Library.

ISBN 1 905204 06 X

Printed in Singapore

PICTURE ACKNOWLEDGEMENTS
The images on the cover and inside pages were all kindly provided by Alamy Limited, with the exception of those on:

pp.24-5,28-9,45,46,50-51,53,54-5,57,96-7,99,102-3,112,122,155,158-9, which were supplied by Getty Images

pp.47,106-7,108,109,118,125,135,136,138,139,156, which were supplied by Freefoto.com

and p.77, which was supplied by Corbis.

The image that appears on pages 158–9 is Dunstanburgh Castle, Northumberland, taken at sunrise.

CONTENTS

INTRODUCTION

As early as 1000 BC, there were enclosures in England that were unmistakably created for military defence. These late bronze age hillforts and their iron age successors were concentric loops of bank and ditch, often laid out on hill tops, and they were apparently intended to function as refuges for whole communities. The most spectacular of these hillforts was Maiden Castle in Dorset, which was the power base of an iron age tribe called the Durotriges (pronounced 'dew-rot-ridge-ease'). Maiden Castle was the stronghold where they made their last stand against the Roman army under Vespasian in AD 43, and where the last defenders were massacred.

Similar earthwork enclosures, often with timber palisades along the banks, were built in the dark ages after the Romans left Britain, at places like Castle Dore and Castle Killibury in Cornwall. These too were serious defensive works, and major community projects.

But none of these fortified enclosures is quite what we now think of as a castle. Above all, we think of a castle as being built of stone. The Romans built in stone, and they raised impressive structures that really were castles. They were remodellings in stone of temporary military camps, rectangular in plan, with an entrance in the centre of each side. Burgh Castle in Suffolk had round towers at the corners and at equidistant points along its walls, looking just like the half-round bastions of a medieval castle.

The Saxons probably built timber castles, and probably on the sites occupied by the Norman castles, but they have been obliterated. We know the Saxons built some fortified palaces at Yeavering and Cheddar; these are rare and precious archaeological survivals because they were not built over later. They were defended by stout palisades, watchtowers and ditches – the bare ingredients of a medieval castle.

Even before the Norman Conquest there was a creeping Normanization. England had an occasional and informal alliance with Normandy against a common foe, the Viking raiders. Edward the Confessor, the penultimate Saxon king of England, had his Norman followers and by 1051 we read that 'the foreigners had built a castle in Herefordshire', perhaps at Hereford itself. We know from documents that at least three castles were built by Normans in England before 1066.

The great age of English castles was launched with the Norman invasion, and for 500 years powerful lords exerted and flaunted their influence through the strength and magnificence of their castles. The castles became mighty symbols of power, virtually defining the middle ages. The great age of English castles came to an end quite suddenly, when the English Civil War showed conclusively that the masonry simply could not stand up to evolving weapons technology. Many were slighted, deliberately disabled to put them out of commission, by Oliver Cromwell. After that, there was a twilight age of nostalgia and romance; the castle ruins came to symbolize a lost age of medieval chivalry. The surviving castles became first mansions, then tourist honeypots and museums.

The great age of castles coincided closely with the great age of cathedrals and abbeys. They too were huge, complex and expensive structures built of stone, the product of a huge communal commitment, and designed to impress. With the abbeys it was not the Civil War that brought about their fall but the greed of Henry VIII a hundred years earlier. Even so, the slighting – and by a neat symmetry it was by that other Cromwell, Thomas Cromwell – had the same effect, of creating picturesque ruins that have become irresistibly romantic symbols of a bygone age.

Windsor Castle (far left) has been home to the Sovereign for over 900 years. Dover Castle (left) saw almost continuous action from the iron age to the Second World War.

ARUNDEL CASTLE

When Duke William of Normandy seized Sussex, he divided it into the six rapes of Chichester, Arundel, Bramber, Lewes, Pevensey and Hastings. Each district commanded a harbour or river mouth; each would have a castle. The 'rape' system seems to have been unique to Sussex, and some think the word means what it says, deriving from the Norman word 'rapiner', to plunder. The ruthless Duke certainly laid waste to much of the county in his effort to create a strong bridgehead for his Norman troops in the event of a Saxon revolt.

After the Conquest, William gave the earldoms of Shrewsbury and Arundel as a reward to Roger de Montgomery, who contributed sixty ships to the invasion fleet. He also ordered Roger to build a castle on the Arun to protect the valley route to the interior.

The origins of Arundel are obscure. What we see today is a heavily reconstructed eighteenth and nineteenth century baronial version of the ancient castle. Local folklore has it that King Alfred fortified the spot, but there is no documentary or archaeological evidence of this.

Whatever was there before, Roger started building his motte and bailey timber fort at Arundel on Christmas Day 1067. He designed it with a motte between two baileys instead of the usual single bailey; he seems to have modelled it on the double bailey plan of Grimboscai in Normandy. The earthworks at Arundel were begun in 1068 and they are still in good condition. The motte is 30m (100ft) high from the bottom of the ditch. The original wooden fort was gradually replaced in stone, starting with the curtain wall and the gatehouse (1070), which is still there, with its original portcullis groove.

Roger de Montgomery died in 1094 and was succeeded by his son Robert, Lord of Belleme. Robert was William II's chief castle-builder. As well as being a hard and cruel warrior, Robert was a 'skilful artificer'. He designed or strengthened not only Arundel but several other castles too – Gloucester, Bridgenorth, Shrewsbury and Tickhill.

Robert rebelled against Henry I in 1102, supporting Henry's brother Robert. He was punished for his disloyalty; Arundel Castle and his lands were taken from him and he was banished for life. After Henry I's death, Arundel passed to his second wife Adelaide of Louvain; in 1138 she married William d'Albini and they made their home at Arundel Castle. D'Albini

owned other lands too and built the splendid square keep at Castle Rising. He was made Earl of Sussex when he married the Queen and he built the stone shell-keep. What William built at Arundel was an outstanding stone shell-keep; others of similar design were Lewes, Cardiff, Restormel, Farnham and Berkeley. The big drum-shaped keep at Arundel Castle was built on an artificial mound. The Domesday Book mentions 49 castles in England, and 28 of them had artificial mottes like Arundel.

The keep was built of Caen stone brought across from Normandy and Quarr Abbey stone from the Isle of Wight. It has smoothly faced walls 8.2m (27ft) high, punctuated by small buttresses.

The year after their marriage in 1139, Adelaide and William invited the Empress Matilda to stay, as she intended to press her claim to the throne from Stephen. Stephen threatened to lay siege to Arundel, so William quickly arranged for her to escape and travel to Bristol. Matilda was unsuccessful in her attempt to gain the throne, but managed to make Stephen agree to her eldest son, Henry II, inheriting it.

When d'Albini died, the castle passed to Henry II, who stayed there in 1182 and on other occasions, spending huge sums on improvements. Under Richard I, Arundel was passed back to the d'Albini family. Then the Fitzalan family took it, and held it until 1555, when the last of the Fitzalans, Mary, married Thomas Howard, Duke of Norfolk, taking Arundel into the Howard family, where it remains.

Richard Fitzalan inherited Arundel in 1272 at the age of five. Richard was a warrior and distinguished himself in the service of Edward I; the two became friends. Richard was described at the Siege of Caerlaverock in 1300, as 'a handsome and well-loved Knight, I saw there richly armed in red with gold lion rampant.' Richard Fitzalan rebuilt the entrance to the keep, the Well Tower and the barbican with two square towers in front of the Norman gateway, which he also heightened.

Richard Fitzalan, the third Earl of Arundel, fought at Crécy with Edward III and the Black Prince. When he returned he provided in his will for the building of the beautiful Fitzalan Chapel. Successive Fitzalans were involved in one war and one royal intrigue after another. John, the seventh Earl, was over six

The Castle Gatehouse built around 1080. The grounds, together with the keep and gatehouse, have been open to the public since 1800 and the gardens since 1854. A large Walled Garden was constructed in the mid-nineteenth century which is currently being restored. It has been planted with standard and fanned apple trees together with rare trees and shrubs.

Richard Fitzalan inherited Arundel in 1272 at the age of five, and is described on the Rolls of the Siege of Caerlaverock in 1300 as:

'A handsome and well-loved Knight, I saw there richly armed in red with gold lion rampant'

feet tall and nicknamed 'the English Achilles'. He was created Duke of Touraine, but then lost his leg at the Battle of Beauvais in 1434 and died of his wound. William Fitzalan, the ninth Earl was Warden of the Cinque Ports.

Thomas Howard, the Duke of Norfolk who took Arundel from the Fitzalans, was beheaded by Elizabeth I for plotting to marry Mary Queen of Scots and having implicit designs on the English throne. His predecessor, the third Duke, was also a plotter; he successfully married off two of his nieces to Henry VIII – Anne Boleyn and Katherine Howard. Both were pawns in the Duke's power play, and both lost their heads. The Duke too was to have lost his head, but Henry VIII died the night before his execution was due to take place, so he was reprieved.

In 1787, the eleventh Duke, Charles Howard, who was a keen architect as well as being a friend of the Prince Regent, decided to reconstruct Arundel Castle to his own design. The works were completed in 1815 at a cost of £600,000. Henry Granville, the fourteenth Duke, started yet another reconstruction, but died before it was finished. The work was finished in 1900, with many internal features of the earlier reconstructions retained. The overall effect is grand and imposing, but the exterior is hard on the eye, because of the excessively smooth finish of the stonework. The castle looks far better when glimpsed from a distance, rising romantically out of the downland beech hangers.

The fifteenth Duke added many modern, twentieth century, touches: electric lights, fire-fighting equipment, service lifts, central heating. The electricity alone cost £36,000 to install. For a long time, the ancient keep was left unrestored, as a picturesque ruin inhabited by a colony of owls.

BATTLE ABBEY

EAST SUSSEX

Now a girls' school, Battle Abbey is entered through a medieval gatehouse that commandingly walls off one end of Battle Market Square. Battle Abbey was famously founded by William the Conqueror to celebrate his conquest of England at the Battle of Hastings on 14 October, 1066. The abbey was built on the site of the battle itself, with the high altar deliberately placed on the spot where King Harold, the last Saxon king, raised his standard as the battle commenced – and where he was later hacked to pieces by Norman knights. It seems an odd act of belated piety on William's part, when immediately after the battle he had the Saxon king's mutilated body buried on the beach, refusing to hand it over to his widow.

Battle Abbey housed Benedictine monks from Marmoutier, near Tours, and was consecrated in 1094. Battle became one of the most prosperous abbeys in England. When the monasteries were dissolved in 1538, it was granted to Sir Anthony Brown, Master of the King's Horse. Brown set about destroying the church and adapting the monastic buildings for his own use.

The gatehouse, built in 1339, is an impressive structure with battlements and turrets, dominating the Market Square and supplying the small town of Battle with its distinctive character. Beyond the gatehouse are various buildings, some still inhabited, such as the Abbot's Lodge, and two towers, which are all that remain of Princess Elizabeth's lodgings. Under the terms of Henry VIII's will, Brown was entrusted with the upbringing of the future queen. Though Brown intended to live at Battle and look after the young princess there, he died in 1548 and the princess never actually went to Battle.

The Abbey Church, 68m (224ft) long, has almost completely vanished, except for part of the undercroft (crypt) of the church's eastern extension, which was erected in the fourteenth century and had five chapels. The foundations are marked out, though, and it is possible to gain from them an impression of the building's size. The chapter house lay to the south of the church's south transept.

Battle Abbey's most impressive remains are the monks' dormitory or dorter, which lies to the south of the site of the Abbey Church and the chapter house. Its undercroft is intact, with its three fine Early English chambers. The lower floor of this building marked the east side of the cloister, while the south wall of the Abbey Church's nave made the cloister's north wall. The remains of a parlour can also be seen between the dorter and the chapter house.

On the south side of the cloister is the frater, with the substantial kitchen beyond. On the west side of the cloister is the abbot's lodge and a range of other buildings, now used as accommodation for the school.

Beyond this complex of buildings there is a very fine broad walk with a splendid view across the valley where the fateful battle took place, still a patchwork of meadows and woods just as it was a thousand years ago. From there it is possible to follow a signed walk with information boards round the battlefield, and imagine the various stages in the Battle of Hastings.

BERKHAMSTED CASTLE

HERTFORDSHIRE

Berkhamsted Castle is a classic example of a Norman motte and bailey castle originally built in timber and later rebuilt in stone. There is a large bailey with fragments of its curtain wall still standing and a large artificial mound, or motte, to one side. There are traces on top of the motte of the foundations of a round stone tower with a rectangular fore-building; there are also wing-walls, which run down the slope of the motte. The bailey is divided into two wards, with a small inner ward at the foot of the motte and the impressive West Tower in the large outer ward.

The most extraordinary feature is the complicated defensive work on the outside of the bailey, where there are two moats separated by a huge earthen rampart. Berkhamsted Castle was built in the late eleventh century at the orders of Robert de Mortain, who was William the Conqueror's half-brother.

Only fragments remain of this once large and important castle. The motte in the north east corner stands 45 feet high and the remains of a complicated arrangement of inner and outer moats can still be seen. William the Conqueror finally accepted the surrender of the Saxons at Berkhamsted, after his defeat of King Harold at Hastings. William the Conqueror was declared King of England at this castle.

In London immediately after the Battle of Hastings, Harold's Saxon heir, Edgar Atheling, was chosen to be king. William the Conqueror decided on a slow progress right round London, devastating the countryside as he went. William intended to starve, isolate and intimidate the Londoners and he was highly successful. After circling London, William quartered himself at Berkhamsted – probably in the Saxon castle that stood on the same site as the Norman castle. A Saxon delegation came out from London, including Morcar, Stigand, Aldred and Edgar himself, to offer William the crown. Then William set off for London for his coronation.

A hundred years after Robert's timber fort was built, Henry II's chancellor and archbishop, Thomas Becket, became its owner. During Becket's time, following the civil war in the reign of King Stephen, the wooden palisades round the motte and bailey were replaced with stone walls. In the reign of King John further defences were added, including wing walls up the slope of the motte and round towers along the bailey curtain wall. These extra defences were put to the test in 1216, when Prince Louis of France laid siege to the castle during an attempt to seize John's crown. The castle fell after an onslaught from giant catapults called mangonels; this attack lasted two weeks.

Later owners of Berkhamsted included Richard Duke of Cornwall, who built Tintagel Castle in Cornwall. It was probably Richard who built the three-storey tower on the western section of the curtain wall. Edward the Black Prince was another owner.

Berkhamsted fell into disuse in 1495 and was never occupied after that. The final indignity came in 1838, when Victorian railway vandals sliced off the south-western edge of the site and demolished the barbican with its rectangular gatehouse to make way for the London and Birmingham Railway. A very similar fate befell Northampton Castle, a fine Norman structure which was demolished to make way for Northampton railway station – a very poor trade-off.

Archaeologists have examined the external earthworks in the twentieth century, and concluded that they were built for King John in the weeks immediately before the 1216 siege.

Berkhamsted Castle is open to the public, but only by prior arrangement with the key-holder.

BODIAM CASTLE

EAST SUSSEX

Bodiam is without a doubt the most beautiful castle in England. It is not only beautifully, almost classically, symmetrical – which satisfies the eye – it is set in the middle of a moat. The moat is so wide that the castle seems like a ship moored in a lake.

That view of the castle across the moat is the best thing about Bodiam. To venture across the causeway and inspect the interior is an anticlimax. The castle is a perfect but hollow shell, as empty as if it had been bombed.

It was in October 1385 that Sir Edward Dalyngrigge was granted a licence by Richard II to fortify his manor house. Both Rye and Winchelsea, ports not far away from Bodiam, had been ravaged by the French within the previous few years. The King was pleased, in his own words, to let Dalyngrigge 'strengthen with a wall of stone and lime, and crenellate and make into a castle his manor house of Bodyham, near the sea, in the county of Sussex, for the defence of the adjacent county, and the resistance to our enemies.'

The wording is odd. Did it mean Kent or Sussex? But Dalyngrigge was not going to abide by the letter of the licence anyway. He pulled down his manor house and built a full-scale stronghold instead. In the event, the castle was never needed as a fortress, and Dalyngrigge might as well have spent his money on a comfortable mansion.

Even so, Sir Edward built modern conveniences into his castle – more than thirty wall fireplaces, a new invention – and it remained a dwelling for a succession of different owners through the fifteenth and sixteenth centuries.

The square castle has a fine round tower at each corner and a square tower projecting from the centre of each wall. The one on the north wall is developed into an elaborate gatehouse, with machicolated towers and a spiked portcullis. Any attacker reaching that point might have boiling oil or pitch poured down on him from the tower's parapets.

One range of buildings was reserved for the mercenary soldiers, regularly employed by the lord of the castle to defend it.

The moat, now only picturesque, was there to defend Bodiam, to supply it with fish, and to dispose of sewage; the castle's garderobes, or lavatories, emptied into it. The moat would have been much less attractive in the middle ages than now. The castle and its way of life would have been a problem to the villagers round about in other ways too. The lord had 300 pairs of pigeons roosting in a tower, and they would have consumed a good proportion of the villagers' crops.

This is a castle without a history. No great events, no battles, no sieges are associated with Bodiam. The only incident was a threat of a siege during the Wars of the Roses, but the Lewknor family surrendered without a fight. Perhaps they did not want their beautiful castle damaged – yet Bodiam remains the quintessence of the English middle ages, and everybody's perfect castle.

CARISBROOKE CASTLE

ISLE OF WIGHT

The poet Keats said, 'I have not seen many specimens of Ruins. I don't think, however, I shall ever see one to surpass Carisbrooke Castle.' If it is in any way unsatisfactory as a Ruin, it is only because it has intact Elizabethan buildings within it. Carisbrooke has some unusual associations; Charles I sat in its window seats, stammering politely to his captors as he looked out across the village, futilely planning his escape.

Carisbrooke is one of the most ancient fortresses in England. A fort probably stood here before the Romans arrived, and when they came they raised a stronghold with a rectangular curtain wall. The Saxons occupied the site after a fierce and bloody battle, and it was probably the Saxons who raised the huge artificial mound which was later to carry the Norman shell-keep.

When the Domesday Survey was undertaken, the mound or motte stood between two baileys enclosed by earthen banks. The first stone structure on the site appears to have been raised in 1136, when Baldwin de Redvers held the Isle of Wight. The shell-keep was built then, and so was the curtain wall surrounding the west bailey.

During the middle ages, Carisbrooke withstood several attacks from the French. The Norman defences remained intact, though the domestic buildings were repeatedly rebuilt and modernized. The great hall and its ancillary buildings were in place by 1299.

The gatehouse, which is the most impressive feature of the castle, was built in 1335, though the beautiful parapets and machicolations were added later, in about 1470. The entrance arch between two stout round towers consists of several arches recessed one within another, creating an effect of enormous solidity. The gatehouse is defended by three portcullises and a moat crossed by a stone bridge.

In the Elizabethan period, the threat from Spain justified extensive improvements. The domestic ranges were brought up to date and some outer defences were added; these ramparts were designed by an Italian engineer, Federigo Gianibelli, Elizabeth I's favourite military designer. It was probably at this time that Carisbrooke Castle's famous well – 60m (200ft) deep – was dug.

The castle was in this upgraded state when Charles I arrived in 1647, optimistically expecting to find sanctuary as well as sympathy from the Governor, Colonel Hammond. It was another of the King's gaffes; Hammond owed his appointment as constable of Carisbrooke to Cromwell – and his father-in-law was John Hampden, another prominent Parliamentarian. Hammond was gracious and subtle, treating the King as a guest at first, then gradually restricting his movements until he was a prisoner. The attempted escape was another fiasco, with the King getting his head stuck between the window bars.

After Charles I lost his head altogether, his two youngest children, Henry Duke of Gloucester and Princess Elizabeth, were also held confined at Carisbrooke Castle, now a state prison, though the thirteen-year-old princess died of a fever within a month. Two years later, the young duke was allowed to leave for the Continent.

Carisbrooke Castle was the Island Governor's residence until 1944. After that the main house was converted into an Isle of Wight Museum.

'I have not seen many specimens of Ruins.
I don't think, however, I shall ever
see one to surpass
Carisbrooke Castle.'
KEATS

COWDRAY HOUSE

WEST SUSSEX

It was on 24 September 1793 that a workman at Cowdray House, a splendid Tudor mansion at the foot of the South Downs near Midhurst, absent-mindedly left a fire unattended. By the end of that day one of the finest houses in Sussex had gone up in smoke. The blaze had penetrated every corner of the building, leaving it a blackened, gutted and roofless shell.

A few weeks after this disaster, the owner of the house, Lord Montague, was attempting to navigate the Rhine Falls at Schaffhausen when he was drowned. This remarkable double disaster was seen by the locals as the fulfilment of a curse put on the Montague family in the sixteenth century by a monk who was expelled from Battle Abbey at the Dissolution of the monasteries in the 1530s, when the abbey was taken over by the Brown family; the head of the Brown family became Viscount Montague.

Founded in 1492 by Sir David Owen, son of Owen Glendower, Cowdray House had, at the time of the fire, been standing for more than 300 years. Like many mansions, Cowdray was modified over the decades by successive owners. Sir William Fitzwilliam made changes after buying the house and estate in 1529. When he died in 1542, the still uncompleted house passed into the hands of his half-brother Sir Anthony Brown, who owned Bayham and Battle Abbeys. Brown was Henry VIII's Master of Horse and one of three unfortunate diplomats entrusted with the task of negotiating the hand of Anne of Cleves for the King, going so far as standing in for the King at the proxy wedding. This involved ceremoniously sliding one white satin-clad leg into Anne's bed as a token bedding on the King's behalf. Perhaps surprisingly, Sir Anthony did not suffer as a result of the King's dislike of Anne of Cleves. When Sir Anthony died in 1548, Cowdray House was complete.

The great park, later landscaped by Capability Brown, was a suitable setting for entertaining royalty. Edward VI was entertained at Cowdray – in fact the young king said that he had been 'rather excessively banqueted there'. Sir Anthony's son, who became the first Lord Montague, entertained Elizabeth I, who never complained that hospitality was too lavish. She shot some of Montague's deer in the park.

But the magnificence of Cowdray all came to an end in 1793. The ruins stand, frozen in their 1793 state, showing still the beautiful Tudor stonework in an impressively consistent, fine, sober, English Renaissance style. Refreshingly, the ruins of Cowdray have not been 'smartened up' in the way that many other historic buildings in England have.

There is a turreted gatehouse, a great hall with huge bay windows and stone transoms and mullions, and many domestic buildings as well, all ranged round a square courtyard. The hall originally had a fine hammerbeam roof of oak timbers; it was known as the Buck Hall because of the life-sized bucks portrayed on the walls bearing shields of England and the Brown family. The Cowdray chapel had a three-sided apse with a large window in each wall and a battlemented roof.

DONNINGTON CASTLE

Donnington Castle is a classic castle ruin of great beauty, one that speaks eloquently both of the medieval spirit and the savagery of the Civil War. This endlessly evocative ruin stands on a hilltop overlooking the River Lambourne, about a mile north of Newbury. It was the home of Sir Richard Abberbury, who acquired a licence to crenellate his property in 1386. Abberbury's licence was granted at the same time as the licence of Edward Dalyngrigge of Bodiam, and he built a castle to a very similar plan to that of Bodiam - but without the all-important moat. Yet even without the moat, Donnington Castle turned out to be one of the most formidable castles ever built in England.

The resulting castle was a rectangular enclosure with a massive round tower at each corner and two square towers or turrets midway along the two longest sides. The curtain wall enclosed the domestic building arranged round a courtyard. The overall design was similar to Bodiam's, but smaller, and it is thought that the domestic buildings may have been built only of timber.

The most impressive part of the castle, and the only part of it that is still standing, was the gatehouse. This three-storey rectangular building has two round towers flanking the entrance. They are incredibly lofty and imposing, rising a full storey above the rest of the gatehouse. One of them has red-brick repairs where a large hole was blasted out by a Parliamentarian mortar in the final attack on the castle in the Civil War.

Legend associates the poet Geoffrey Chaucer with Donnington Castle, but there is no proof that he ever visited it. Abberbury sold Donnington to Thomas, Chaucer's son, but he in turn sold it to Sir John Phelipp, his son-in-law. Princess Elizabeth later owned the castle, and spent some time there in fearful retirement while her dangerous half-sister Mary Tudor was on the throne.

Donnington Castle was seized by Royalist forces during the Civil War following the Battle of Newbury. Captain John Boys was put in charge of defending it. He raised a set of earthworks round the castle in the form of a star, which successfully withstood a Parliamentary siege in 1644. Charles I took an army to relieve Donnington Castle and the second Battle of Newbury was fought round it.

This time the King's troops were forced to retreat, but Colonel Boys bravely refused to surrender the castle. Boys managed to secure the Royalist munitions inside the castle, and the King himself came and took them away ten days after the battle, without the Parliamentarian officers knowing he was there. The second siege, led by Colonel Horton, continued for an incredible eighteen months. Then Boys finally accepted terms for a conditional surrender, but only after continual heavy bombardment had reduced the castle to an almost total ruin. He and his 200-strong garrison were allowed to march out of the castle unimpeded and rejoin the Royalist army at Wallingford. Boys was knighted by the King; he deserved it.

The earthworks raised in the Civil War can still be seen round the castle, which is very much 'one of the ruins that Cromwell knocked about a bit'.

The most impressive part of Donnington Castle, and indeed the only part now standing, was the gatehouse. This is a three-storey rectangular building with two round towers that flank the entrance and rise another storey above the rest of the building.

DOVER CASTLE

KENT

Although some keeps in the 1180s were being built in the new, experimental cylindrical shape, Dover Castle was given an old-fashioned square keep, even though it would have blind and vulnerable corners. Dover's keep was a big cube, surrounded by a long curtain wall with fourteen square towers and two powerful gatehouses. It cost £6,000. The keep was fitted with an ingenious plumbing system, but the overall architectural design showed no advance on the square keeps built fifty years earlier, such as the White Tower at London.

Dover, like other castles, took a long time to build. The stonework of the keep probably grew at a rate of only 3m (10ft) per season, which usually meant March to October. A keep 18.3m (60ft) high would therefore have taken six years to build. It was important to get the design right because of the cost in time, manpower and money, so it is strange that Dover was built to a design that would be obsolete when finished. It may be that Henry II was confident that the square keep would be secure within the outer defence system, which did incorporate innovations; it had immensely strong wall-towers and gatehouses. The projecting wall-towers effectively prevented the walls from being mined, because they could provide fire cover for every inch of the wall. With a really strong curtain wall, the strength of the keep became less important. The square designs were much easier to build and from a domestic point of view easier to live in. Henry II and his half-brother Hamelin evidently had different views on military architecture. Henry built Dover while Hamelin built Conisbrough.

The Angevin kings spent a huge amount of money on castles, and evidently believed their thrones depended on them. Between 1155 and 1215, they spent £46,000 on building castles. This amounted to almost one-tenth of their revenues. Henry II spent £21,000 on his castles, of which Dover was one. Richard I by contrast spent little on English castles, apart from the £3,000 he spent on the Tower of London. John spent £1,000 a year on castles, mainly adding, repairing, and strengthening existing castles. Henry III spent £85,000 in all on castles, about one-tenth of his annual income. He allocated £7,500 to updating Dover Castle. These outlays may look extravagant, but neither Henry II nor John enjoyed spending money. It was simply that they recognized the need to defend themselves against untrustworthy barons. Henry II was also keen to force lesser barons out of the arms race; the fewer castle-owning barons there were, the more easily he could deal with them. During this phase, many lesser barons had to content themselves with a new type of residence, the moated manor-house. This was an adequate defence against casual local rebellion, but not against a determined attack. By raising the stakes, Henry II cleverly saved himself money. Overall, there were fewer castles in England, and as a result fewer royal castles were needed.

One significant innovation Henry's engineers introduced at Dover was a new kind of wall aperture – arrow-slits for crossbows in the Avranches Tower.

HASTINGS CASTLE

EAST SUSSEX

After landing in Sussex in 1066, Duke William of Normandy raised two castles on the south coast in rapid succession. It was a matter of urgency to secure his bridgehead in England and defend his position. The Norman fleet had landed in Pevensey Bay, so it was natural to strengthen the old Roman fort of Pevensey itself first, to protect his fleet from the west. Then he had a castle built on the cliffs at Hastings, to protect his army from the east. While these building works were going on, King Harold's Saxon army was marching south to engage him in battle. Hastings Castle was completed shortly before the great and decisive battle.

These two castles were built fast, out of timber, and William brought them with him in prefabricated kit form, in his ships. The Norman invasion was nothing if not well-planned.

Duke William was crowned King of England on Christmas Day, 1066. By 1070, the new King had issued orders that the castle of Hastings, together with the newly built St Mary's Chapel, should be rebuilt in stone. It was the Count of Eu who held the castle at Hastings through the Norman period.

At one point, King John gave orders for Hastings Castle to be slighted to stop it falling into the hands of the French. In around 1220, Henry III ordered the re-fortification of the castle and it then flourished for 60 years.

In 1287, disaster struck. There were many months of severe weather. Great storms ravaged the coastline and huge waves attacked and undermined the sandstone cliffs. Huge sheets of rock collapsed into the sea, taking sections of the castle with them. There were other environmental changes too. There was deforestation and more extensive ploughing in the Weald. This released tonnes of silt into the rivers, and they in turn dumped the silt in the river-mouth harbours. Many south coast ports, such as Steyning and Seaford, suffered a decline. Hastings suffered in the same way, with the castle abandoned and the town impoverished.

In 1339 and 1377, when England was at war with France, Hastings was attacked by the French and badly damaged. Through

In the mid-sixteenth century Hastings Castle received its final blow when Henry VIII dissolved the monasteries. His commissioners seized the land, lead, bells and anything else of value, leaving the now exposed buildings to decay.

The majestic ruins of the castle command panoramic views of the town, and include such features as the 'whispering Dungeons', and the once magnificent Eastern Gateway where you can still see the slots for the portcullis.

the next hundred years, coastal erosion meant that even more of the castle was lost to the sea. In the sixteenth century, Hastings Castle was dealt a final blow when the monasteries were dissolved. Henry VIII's commissioners seized land, lead and anything else of value, and left the exposed ruins to decay.

The land was bought by the local Pelham family and used for farming. The scant remains of the neglected castle and church became so overgrown that people actually forgot they were there. In 1824, they were rediscovered and excavated. Several coffins were found. The surviving walling was repaired and a section of the north wall and a church arch were rebuilt. In this partially revived condition, the place became a popular attraction for Victorian visitors to the seaside town. In the Second World War some stray bombs added further damage to the almost total ruin.

HERSTMONCEUX CASTLE

EAST SUSSEX

Herstmonceux Castle is unusual in being a fairly late creation. It was Sir Roger Fiennes who was granted a licence to crenellate in 1441. Herstmonceux is also unusual in being built of Flemish brick, and it was one of the first great buildings to be brick-built. Brick is, of course, more suited to house-building than castle-building.

Herstmonceux (pronounced 'Hurstman-soo') was built in a lake, so that the water could function as a moat. The water also had the effect of providing a reflection of the castle and making it appear loftier than it was. The aptly named Fiennes was Treasurer to the Household of Henry VI, and he was rich enough and of high enough status to build himself a truly splendid house. It was not always enough to be rich. Rank dictated what people were allowed to do. Rank dictated what colours and what fabrics they could and could not wear; there were sumptuary laws to control these signs of rank. Only a very high court official would have dared to commission so grand a mansion as Herstmonceux.

The most striking feature of the castle is the gatehouse with its two imposing two-tiered towers – almost too medieval to be true – rising 26 metres (84 feet) on either side of the entrance arch and drawbridge. The long frontage stretching away on each side has something of Hampton Court Palace about it. The impression is all too telling; these brick walls would never have withstood a cannon ball, let alone an artillery bombardment. Luckily they were never put to the test.

The large square castle with its many towers and chimneys is nevertheless a very impressive sight. Its interior was well-appointed, and designed more for comfort than defence. Herstmonceux was always more a mansion than a fortress.

Unfortunately some of the castle's later owners did not invest enough in maintenance. By the close of the eighteenth century, quite a lot of its fabric had been taken away by the Revd Robert Hare to be used as building materials for his new house, nearby Herstmonceux Place. This action reduced Herstmonceux to a ruin.

In the early twentieth century, the castle was resurrected by Sir Claude Lowther. By referring back to the original plans, the ruins were transformed back into an impressive home and the fine red brick exterior of the castle was faithfully restored to its original state. This work was carried out by Sir Paul Latham.

In 1946, Herstmonceux became the home of the Royal Greenwich Observatory, which escaped from the London smogs to exploit the cleaner air of the countryside and the lack of light pollution. The Observatory remained at Herstmonceux for forty years before moving on in 1989, but the old Equatorial Telescope Buildings remain open to the public as an educational centre. The castle as a whole is a conference centre in private hands and not always open to the public, but guided tours are available by appointment. There are extensive gardens round the castle, and these too are open to the public at certain times of the year.

HEVER CASTLE

KENT

As we see in the story of Dover Castle, Henry II deliberately accelerated the arms race, making state-of-the-art castle-building such an expensive business that only a small elite of barons could afford to stay in the race. The stragglers, the poorer barons, had to content themselves with fortified manor houses. In the two centuries following Henry II's reign, the thirteenth and fourteenth centuries, many of these lesser barons built themselves fine houses that would withstand casual attack. Many of these have been lost and only their moats remain in the rural landscape to remind us of their former presence. A few have survived and been restored.

One outstanding example of these survivors is Hever Castle. Its first licence to crenellate is dated 1340, but the creation of the moat we see today and the main defences evidently came after a second licence was granted, in 1384, to Sir John de Cobham. The main motive for investing money in defence at that time was almost certainly the threat of a French invasion of south-east England. The defensive works were nevertheless maintained right through the fifteenth century, and it is likely that the occupants of Hever were fearful of predatory neighbours in Kent itself, the likes of Lord Saye and Sele.

In 1462, Hever Castle was acquired by Sir Geoffrey Boleyn, a successful hatter who became Lord Mayor of London.

The most impressive feature of Hever Castle is the colossal three-storeyed gatehouse, which seems far too big for this modest little castle. It is a high medieval take on the Norman keep, with drawbridge, portcullis, elaborate – and probably decorative – machicolation and battlements. There is also some decorative carved stonework above the gate and a pleasantly asymmetrical arrangement of windows, large and small. It is a very pretty building, but it would be vain to suppose that it would ever have withstood cannon-fire.

The best that Hever could have resisted was a smash-and-grab attempt at burglary. This type of raid did occur. An example is the attack by Lord Moleyns on Gresham in 1448.

Margaret Paston described it: 'A thousand of Moleyns' followers turned up 'arrayed in manner of war, cuirasses, coats of mail, steel helmets, bows, shields, ladders and picks with which they mined down the walls, and long trees with which they broke up gates and doors, and so came into the said mansion . . . and rifled and bare away stuff, array and money to the value of £200.'

This was famously the scene of Henry VIII's courtship of one of the daughters of the house, Anne Boleyn, a bitter-sweet historical association that still hangs heavy on the air at Hever.

The Astor family took ownership of the castle, and undertook its restoration and modernization, turning it into a very comfortable home. Who would not want to live in a house with such a perfect library, lit by sunlight reflected in from a moat through leaded panes? The restoration work began in 1903 and cost a great deal of money. Part of the work involved landscaping the grounds. This included the creation of an artificial lake; a team of local labourers was hired to dig out the lake. Looking at the lake now, the labourers long gone, it is hard to believe that any human hand was involved in its creation.

This thirteenth century romantic castle was once the childhood home of Anne Boleyn. The spectacular gardens were laid out between 1904 and 1908 by Joseph Cheal & Son, turning what was once marshland into the magnificent gardens you see today. One of the most magnificent areas of the gardens is the Italian Garden, which was designed to display William Waldorf Astor's collection of Italian sculpture.

LEEDS CASTLE

Kent

Like Bodiam, Leeds Castle is a fairytale castle that seems to float on a great lake. It was built in 857 by Ledian, the chief minister of Ethelbert IV, King of Kent, who saw the lake formed by the River Len, with the two islands in the middle, as a perfect site for his castle. Ledian built a wooden fort on the two islands. Ethelbert, it was said, 'governed with love and honour'; one of its more recent owners said that Leeds Castle was always 'a happy castle'.

In common with many Anglo-Saxon castles, it has been forgotten, but the Norman invaders quickly recognized the value of the site. William I gave Leeds to his half-brother, Bishop Odo of Bayeux. When Odo rebelled, William took the castle back and granted it to Hamon de Crevecour, who had fought with the King at Hastings. De Crevecour started building the stone castle in the reign of Henry I, in 1119. The family was very pious, perhaps because of a curse that hung over them.

For over 200 years the castle stayed in the de Crevecour family. Hamon, the great-grandson of Robert de Crevecour, was one of the rebel barons in the reign of King John. In the reign of Henry III he became Warden of the Cinque Ports. His son Robert fought against Henry III and when the King decisively won the Battle of Evesham the family fortunes went into a steep decline. The de Crevecours were forced to give up Leeds Castle, which the King granted to one of his devoted supporters, Sir Roger de Leyburn. Both Roger and his son William were great soldiers and loyal to the crown; William gave his castle to Edward I in 1278.

Edward I and his queen loved Leeds Castle, using it much as the present royal family uses Balmoral. The King spent a lot of money extending the castle. Until this time, the defence of the castle depended mainly on the lake. On the islands themselves, there was little in the way of defensive work. Edward I decided that this was unsatisfactory and added a high bastioned outer wall to make an outer bailey, a barbican and the Gloriette, a D-shaped tower functioning as a mini-fortress on the smaller island. The new walls rose straight out of the water. The gatehouse was also enlarged.

Edward I, unusually, loved his wife, Eleanor of Castile – it was not a mere dynastic marriage – and gave the perfected Leeds Castle to her as a present. He routinely addressed Eleanor, in French, as 'Chère Reine', 'dear queen'. The cross he raised in London to her on her death was known as 'Chère Reine Croix', or Charing Cross. When the King remarried, he gave Leeds Castle to his second

When you get to the centre of the Maze at Leeds Castle, you don't have to find your way back out again, instead, you follow the signs and enter a doorway under the central mound, which leads down into the Grotto. This Grotto travels underground through stone passageways where you will see the famous Stone Face (above).

wife, Margaret. This association led to Leeds being nicknamed the Ladies Castle.

Edward II granted Leeds Castle to Lord Badlesmere. When Queen Isabella called to stay the night in the summer of 1321, she was testing Badlesmere's loyalty. Walter Culpeper was constable of the castle. He was bold enough to refuse Queen Isabella entry to the castle, advising her to 'seek some other lodging'. 'The Captain most malapertly repulsed her, insomuch that she complained grievously to the King', Edward II, who laid siege to the castle in the November, used ballistas or springalds and an army of 30,000 men to force a surrender. 'Then he tooke Captaine Colepeper and hoong him up'. Lord Badlesmere was sent to the Tower and later beheaded. In 1327, Queen Isabella took the castle for herself, and kept it until her death in 1358.

Edward III carried out many repairs. The chambers of the King and Queen in the Gloriette were improved and a new garderobe especially for the King was installed.

In 1395, the French historian Froissart met Richard II at Leeds Castle; Froissart mentions it in his Chronicles. 'I shewd not the kynge the boke that I hadde brought for hym, he was so sore occupied with great affayres.' At this time, the clerk of works at Leeds Castle was none other than Henry Yevele, the great architect who was responsible for the roof of Westminster Hall and the astonishingly beautiful nave at Canterbury Cathedral, the finest piece of medieval architecture in England.

Henry IV, who took Richard's throne, gave Leeds to his wife, Queen Joan of Navarre. They spent the summer of 1403 there to avoid the plague in London. In 1412, Joan gave the castle to Thomas Arundel, Archbishop of Canterbury. It was to Leeds Castle that the Archbishop summoned Sir John Oldcastle to stand trial for heresy.

The sixth and last queen to receive Leeds as a dower from her husband was Catherine de Valois, Henry V's queen. She acquired it in 1423, installing a clock and bell in 1435. The bell was last rung on the Queen's visit to Leeds Castle in 1985. When Henry V died, Catherine was still only 21. She fell in love with Owen Tudor, the Welshman who was Clerk of the Queen's Wardrobe, looking after her dresses and jewels. Leeds Castle seems a perfect setting for this remarkable romance between the 'dowager' queen and her servant. When their affair was discovered they were imprisoned, but Owen Tudor escaped and Catherine was released. They had, however, been secretly married. Their son, Edmund, became the father of Henry VII.

Henry VIII was the most famous owner of Leeds Castle. He liked Leeds very much, often visited and spent huge sums enlarging and improving the building.

He in effect turned Leeds Castle from a fortress into a palace. The Maidens' Tower was built for the visit of Henry VIII's first queen, to house her maids of honour. Among those maids was Anne Boleyn, from nearby Hever Castle.

Henry VIII gave Leeds to Sir Anthony St Leger, and the castle passed out of royal ownership. Eventually, in 1929, the castle was bought by Lady Olive Baillie. She completely restored the building again and lived in it longer than any other owner; once again Leeds became a lady's castle. In the Second World War, Lady Baillie offered the castle as a military hospital, and it became a convalescent home for airmen with severe burns. She finally left Leeds to the nation.

Leeds Castle, the Ladies Castle, flies the flags of two ladies alternately – Eleanor of Castile, the first lady owner, and Lady Baillie, the last.

LEWES CASTLE

EAST SUSSEX

Lewes Castle was founded by William de Warenne, one of Duke William of Normandy's followers. De Warenne was rewarded with lands in Sussex, Surrey and Norfolk; he built castles at Reigate and Castle Acre, but his main focus was Lewes, where he built the castle that would be his family's residence for almost three hundred years.

De Warenne decided to visit Rome with his wife Gundrada, but they stopped in Burgundy, where they visited the Abbey of Cluny. It was due to this visit that, on his return, de Warenne founded a Cluniac priory at Lewes. Gundrada was buried in their new priory in 1085. De Warenne himself died in 1088 and was buried beside his wife.

Lewes was an important Saxon township before the Normans arrived. The medieval town walls probably follow the line of Saxon defences and the street plan is almost certainly inherited from the Saxon period. Possibly a Saxon castle formerly stood on the site of de Warenne's castle.

Lewes Castle is unusual in having two chalk mottes or castle mounds, Brack Mount to the north-east and the keep mound to the south-west, one at each end of a level oval bailey. Late in the eleventh century an oval shell keep was raised on the south-western mound. A rectangular gatehouse was built to make an entrance on the south and the court or bailey was surrounded with a flint-faced wall. Surviving wall fragments show courses of large flints laid in a herring-bone pattern, typical of early Norman masonry.

The keep has been partially destroyed. The walls on the north and east sides have gone. There have also been modifications to turn it into a kind of folly. The porch and circular stair to the south tower are all nineteenth century. The very attractive projecting towers were added much earlier, in the thirteenth century. There was probably an entrance tower on the east side.

The southern tower is quite well preserved. In the nineteenth century, Mr Kemp cut the arrow loops to put in 'Gothic' windows, though these in their turn have been replaced by square openings. A second storey has been inserted. The roof and parapets are modern. In spite of all this modern interference, it is still worth going up the tower for the sake of the splendid view of the town of Lewes and the Brookland beyond.

On the north side of the keep was a sally port, which probably led to a door in the town wall below.

The fine barbican or outer gatehouse built in the fourteenth century is by far the best feature of Lewes Castle. Barbicans were frequently left unroofed and in effect no more than fortified bridges with gates. The Lewes barbican nevertheless has a roof. It stands three storeys tall, with two round towers defending the southern entrance. They are linked at the top by a line of machicolations. The flintwork is very high quality, of squared knapped flint, and a fine early example of this kind of masonry.

Much of Lewes Castle was pulled down in the 1600s for building stone but the impressive fourteenth century Barbican Gatehouse remains (right).

PEVENSEY CASTLE

EAST SUSSEX

Pevensey is a really remarkable place – two very different castles for the price of one, and sitting one within the other. In the Roman period, on the site of the broad flat land of Pevensey Levels between the sites of Eastbourne and Bexhill, there was a large shallow bay. Its coastline was irregular, and a slim peninsula projected into the middle of it from the west. It was on this natural jetty, which was virtually an island in the shallow bay, that the Romans built one of their most impressive forts. This was Anderida. It was built in the third century AD to defend the so-called Saxon Shore, the coastline of England most at threat from Saxon colonization.

The Roman builders went to some trouble to make secure foundations for this fortress in the marsh, creating a bed of clay and flints 4.6m (15ft) wide. On top of this they placed oak beams set in concrete. Then, on top of that, they raised the massive curtain wall, 3.7m (12ft) thick and almost 9.1m (30ft) high. It was made of mortared flint rubble faced with stone, with courses of tile running along it.

'And my dear Lord, if it like you to know my fare, I am here laid by in manner of a siege . . . so that I may not out nor no victuals get me, but with much hard.'

LADY JANE PELHAM

(She defended the castle while her husband was away fighting in northern England.)

This Roman curtain wall was an immense structure, punctuated with squat round towers or bastions, and it enclosed a huge area of more than 3.2 hectares (8 acres). Most incredibly of all, this magnificent fortress still stands intact after sixteen hundred years, even though it has seen repeated military action and has been besieged several times over.

The first attack on Anderida that we know about is recorded in the Anglo-Saxon Chronicle. In the fifth century, Aelle, the first Saxon King of Sussex, and his son Cissa laid siege to Andredeceaster (the fort of Anderida), 'and slew all the inhabitants; there was not even one Briton left there'. Evidently the local Britons had taken refuge in the old Roman fort, but Aelle ruthlessly massacred them regardless. This merciless and decisive rout firmly established Aelle as the unchallenged King of Sussex and, along with other victories such as a battle at Seaford, his reputation was such that he emerged as the first 'bretwalda', or commander-in-chief, of the Anglo-Saxons.

The walls of the Roman fortress were still complete when Duke William of Normandy sailed his invasion fleet into Pevensey Bay 600 years later. The Conqueror occupied the magnificent old fort and immediately erected his

Originally a Roman fortress, Pevensey Castle saw its share of violence in the middle ages. During the four centuries after William the Conqueror landed here, it was attacked and besieged many times.

very first English timber castle inside it. It is said that he brought this first timber castle across in kit form in his ships. The fine old Roman walls of Anderida made a perfect outer bailey, and indeed may even have suggested a blueprint for later English castles built from scratch that were to follow.

In time, the initial early Norman timber castle was replaced by a stone late Norman castle. This happened after Robert of Mortain, William's half-brother, had been granted Pevensey. The inner defences gradually took shape round the Norman keep during the thirteenth century; these consisted of a moat, a wall and a gatehouse with two towers. The new curtain wall of the inner bailey was built in architectural imitation of the Roman curtain wall by having three D-shaped towers, just like the Roman bastions.

Pevensey both triumphed and failed defensively. For example, William Rufus starved Pevensey into surrender, but King Stephen and Simon de Montfort both laid siege to Pevensey and failed to make it yield. At the close of the fourteenth century, Pevensey was once again successfully defended, this time by Lady Jane Pelham against the allies of the deposed Richard II; her husband was away fighting in the north of England. Lady Jane wrote to her husband, 'And my dear Lord, if it like you to know my fare, I am here laid by in manner of a siege. . . so that I may not out nor no victuals get me, but with much hard.'

By 1400, Pevensey Castle was no longer standing in a bay but in a saltmarsh. The shingle spit known as the Crumbles was building gradually across the entrance to the bay and turning it into an increasingly sheltered expanse of marsh. Pevensey, like some other south coast ports – Steyning, Rye and Winchelsea – was being left behind by the sea, thanks to accelerating silting. As a result, Pevensey was gradually losing its importance as a coastal fortress.

It was, even so, fortified against the Spanish Armada in 1588. A gun called a demi-culverin, and made of local Wealden iron, still stands within the castle's inner bailey. Even during the Second World War the location was seen as having a strategic significance, and gun emplacements were built to defend this stretch of coastline against a landing of German tanks and infantry. But the fabric of the castle itself had long since fallen into rack and ruin. In the seventeenth century, when the Parliamentary commissioners surveyed it, Pevensey Castle was already in a state of neglect. Curiously, the Roman walls are now in a rather better state than the Norman walls, even though they are about a thousand years older.

Many medieval castles were made very comfortable, but Pevensey seems to have remained fairly austere. Domestic considerations had to give way to the requirements of military strength. Pevensey had relatively few garderobes and the accommodation was really sub-medieval. Here it was that the young Thomas Becket was sent as a boy by his father, to learn the ways of gentlemen; it was customary in the middle ages to send upper class boys away to be schooled in a castle belonging to a stranger – the precursor of the English public school system. Pevensey must have been a particularly hard school for the young Becket.

Pevensey Castle is a wonderfully tangible link with several epoch-making episodes in English history; with the Roman conquest, with the threat and the actuality of the Saxon invasion, with the emergence of a pan-Saxon war-leader, with the Norman invasion and the consolidation of that conquest, with the boyhood of England's greatest medieval saint, with the threatened Spanish and German invasions, and above all with the shifting shape of the coastline of England.

The ruins of the medieval castle at Pevensey stand in one corner of a Roman fort, on what was once a peninsula surrounded by the sea and salt marshes.

ROCHESTER CASTLE

KENT

Rochester's Norman keep is an uncompromisingly aggressive building, raw, externally undecorated, and as rough as a sea-cliff.

It was in 1088 that William Rufus persuaded Gundulf to build a high stone curtain wall round the bailey at Rochester, to make the wooden keep more secure. The King and his bishop shared the cost of what was an expensive new structure that would be useful to both of them, improving the security of both city and state. It guarded Rochester and the important Medway river crossing on the London-Dover road, a key strategic site that had been fortified in Roman times. It was the gifted Gundulf who had designed the White Tower, the massive keep at Colchester and the half-sized keep at Canterbury. The wooden keep at Rochester, however, was not to be rebuilt in stone until Henry I's time. In 1125, Henry I entrusted Archbishop William of Corbeuil with Rochester Castle and gave him permission to build an *egregium turrim* in place of the now obsolete wooden keep.

What the archbishop built was indeed 'an outstanding tower'. When complete, thirteen years later, it rose through five floors to a height of 38m (125ft), making it the tallest keep in England. It was built with walls 3.7m (12ft) thick made of Kentish ragstone and Caen stone facings. It was intended to be an imposing, even menacing, building. It still is today. Of all the Norman castles in England, Rochester speaks loudest of the brutality and oppression that followed the Norman conquest.

A forebuilding gave external access to the keep at first floor level. A partition wall divided the keep into two equal halves. This wall was pierced by round arches decorated with carved chevrons and supported by thin round columns. There was a well-shaft running right up through the building, so that water was independently available on every floor. There was also a stone newel staircase rising to the roof. There were only small windows, but fireplaces ensured that the rooms were not filled with smoke.

In 1215, in the reign of King John, Rochester Castle withstood a ferocious three-month siege. The defenders were able to continue fighting even after John's soldiers had broken into the tower, surrendering only after they ran out of food. According to a contemporary chronicler, when this most impregnable of fortresses fell, 'men no longer put their trust in castles'. Rochester was the peak of development of the great square keep. Others followed, such as Hedingham, but in pale imitation and often already with a 'retro' feeling about them. Their weakness lay in their corners, which could be prised apart by attackers with crowbars.

During the Hundred Years War, Rochester, though now very out of date, was refortified, with an eye on a possible attack by the French on the Thames estuary.

By 1561 the grand old tower-keep was but a relic from a bygone age. Stone from the old Norman curtain wall was taken to build a new castle at Upnor, opposite the naval base at Chatham.

Yet Rochester still had influence. When the Welsh slate millionaire George Dawkins-Pennant had a Norman Revival castle-mansion built, from 1827 onwards, he built a square keep 35m (115ft) high – and modelled it on Rochester.

TOWER OF LONDON

The Raven Master at the Tower of London. The Ravens are one of The Tower's most famous sights. These magnificent birds have lived within its walls for hundreds of years and legend has it that, if they leave, the kingdom will fall.

Most of the first-generation castles built after the Norman Conquest were made of timber; only later was stone used. The Tower of London was built in stone from the start. The Romans decided that the river crossing was important enough to defend with a fort and then an enclosing wall, which eventually became the wall of the City of London. The city then needed to be defended against possible invasion from the sea, which meant building a fortress at the point where the seaward end of the city wall reached the Thames. This was where William the Conqueror built his greatest castle.

The site may have an even longer ancestry. There is a tradition that Julius Caesar was the founder of the Tower, and archaeologists partially confirm this by finding traces of Roman fortifications under the medieval walls.

In the years immediately after Hastings, William's aim was to build as many small timber motte-and-bailey castles as he could defend, mostly overlooking towns. Between 1066 and 1071, castles sprang up at Lincoln, Chester, Stafford, Tutbury, Shrewsbury, Wisbech, Norwich, Huntingdon, Worcester, Clifford, Hereford, Ewyas Harold, Cambridge, Oxford, Monmouth, Pevensey, Winchester, Dover, Hastings, York – and London. The Domesday Book of 1086-7 mentions 49 castles as existing at that time. Of the 49 listed, 33 were standing on sites that had already been fortified before 1066. This means that many of the castles credited to William the Conqueror were remodelled Saxon or even older castles. Portchester Castle has a square Norman keep in the corner of a square Roman fort. At Pevensey, a square Norman keep stands rather oddly within an elliptical Roman curtain wall.

The magnificent White Tower at the Tower of London was the very finest of these great square keeps. It was built of ragstone rubble with ashlar dressings, walls between 3.7m (12ft) and 4.6m (15ft) feet thick at the base and 27m (90ft) high – the corner turrets rising even higher. There were also projections formed by the end of the chapel and the staircase.

William Rufus added an inner bailey between the White Tower and the Thames. This was later destroyed. A middle bailey was created in 1190 and a Bell Tower in the Plantagenet period. In 1300 Edward I completed the outer bailey, the moat, three outer gates and a barbican. Throughout all these changes and later developments, the core of the castle remained the imposing keep designed by Gundulf, the talented Bishop of Rochester, and completed in 1078.

44

The curtain wall of the Tower encloses a large irregular hexagon, which is surrounded by a substantial moat which is now dry, though there are plans to flood it again. Two lines of fortifications enclose the inner bailey, where the White Tower stands. The walls of the White Tower were restored by Christopher Wren, but in Norman style, and all is Norman within.

Among the surrounding buildings are a nineteenth century barracks – the Tower was still garrisoned until modern times – and the Chapel of St Peter ad Vincula, which was built in the twelfth century but remodelled in the fourteenth and sixteenth centuries.

The Ballium Wall is the inner of the two lines of fortification and dates from the same time as the keep. Studding the Ballium Wall at intervals are thirteen towers. One is the Wakefield Tower, where for a long time the crown jewels were kept and displayed. This was also the oratory where the deposed Henry VI was kept prisoner and also where he was killed, in 1471, on the orders of Edward IV.

The main entrance to the Tower is through the Middle Tower in the west. Beside it there was a menagerie or zoo from Norman times right through to the nineteenth century. Access is by way of a bridge over the moat and then through the Byward Tower.

On the south, giving entry to the Tower from the river through St Thomas's Tower and the Bloody Tower, is the famous Traitor's Gate. Prisoners of rank were usually conducted to the Tower by river rather than through the streets of London, and they were delivered to the steps under the menacing low arch of this gate. It is not open to the river any longer because of the increasing risk of tidal flooding; an embankment bars access today. The great interest the Tower of London holds for us today is its connection over several centuries with distinguished prisoners and their fateful executions, often by public beheading, sometimes by secret assassination.

The Beauchamp Tower was for a long time the main place of confinement for high-ranking prisoners, but there are chambers and dungeons all over the Tower complex that are associated with one prisoner or another. The Bell Tower accommodated Princess Elizabeth, Bishop Fisher and Sir Thomas More. The Bowyer Tower was the prison of the Duke of Clarence, the treacherous brother of Edward IV and Richard III. Shakespeare had Richard III as

Clarence's murderer, but it was Edward IV who had Clarence executed, and it was Clarence himself who asked to die by being ducked head-first into a butt of Malmsey.

The Salt Tower and the Broad Arrow Tower were the places where the Catholic prisoners of Queen Elizabeth I's reign were incarcerated. The Martin Tower was where Colonel Blood carried out his almost-successful attempt to steal the crown jewels, which at that time were kept there.

Executions were carried out both within the Tower and very publicly on Tower Hill. An area marked out on Tower Green is shown to tourists as the site of the block, but the scaffold was normally erected in the open space to the south of the White Tower. Many of those executed were buried in the Chapel of St Peter ad Vincula, such as Sir Thomas More, Queen Anne Boleyn, Queen Katharine Howard, Lady Jane Grey and the Duke of Monmouth.

The association of the Tower with high-profile prisoners such as Sir Walter Raleigh tends to put a heavy emphasis on the Tower as a prison. It certainly continued to be a prison through the nineteenth century, and was even used occasionally as a military prison in the twentieth century. The last prisoners were the Kray twins, who were imprisoned there briefly following their arrest as army deserters.

The Tower was not just a prison and a fortress, though. It was a royal palace, from at least the reign of King Stephen until the time of Oliver Cromwell. The Tower continues to be a fortress of sorts, policed by Yeomen Warders, known as 'Beefeaters', who wear Tudor uniforms.

Because of the part it has played in so many significant episodes of English history, the Tower has become a potent symbol of English history. To understand fully all the things that have happened within its still-forbidding walls is to understand the history of England itself.

WALMER CASTLE

Unlike castles of an earlier medieval date, Walmer Castle has no high walls for protection. The concentric plan of the castle was typical of Henry VIII's castles being built of stone and brick, with a circular keep located at its centre. Surrounding the keep is a circular curtain wall with four, almost circular, bastions projecting from it. Access to the castle was via a bridge and drawbridge at the northern bastion, which acted as the castle's gatehouse.

Walmer Castle belongs to the major refortification programme set in motion by Henry VIII. There was a major invasion scare in 1538, when the Pope succeeded in reconciling Henry's two Catholic enemies, the Holy Roman Emperor Charles V and the French King Francis I. Suddenly England was faced with the prospect of an imminent joint Imperial-French invasion. Lambarde, the Elizabethan historian of Kent, wrote that Henry VIII, 'determined to stand upon his own guard and defence; and without sparing any cost he builded castles, platforms and blockhouses in all needful places of the Realm.'

Within just two years, Henry had accomplished an amazing feat; he had built the first comprehensive new defence system of southern Britain since Roman times. The Thames was fitted with five new forts. Next came three new castles intended to protect the anchorage in the

Downs – Sandown (now mostly eroded away by the sea), Deal and Walmer. Next came the set of four new castles to defend the Solent – Calshot and Hurst on the mainland, East and West Cowes on the Isle of Wight. Finally came the new castle at Portland. The overall scheme protected the English coast from the Thames estuary to Dorset, and it was almost entirely in place by 1540 – a remarkable achievement.

The design of these new-generation castles was very distinct, with an emphasis on huge round low bastions, yet there were elements that were inherited from the Norman castles too. Each had a central round tower, corresponding to the Norman keep; that central tower stood in a bailey with a bastioned curtain wall; it also had a moat. At Walmer, the circular curtain wall was only a little larger than the central tower, and it was dominated by its four huge bastions. Walmer Castle was similar in plan to Deal Castle, though smaller and with four bastions instead of Deal's six. It is not known how many guns Walmer carried in Henry's day, but by 1597 it was equipped with one cannon, one culverin, five demi-culverins, a saker, a minion and a falcon. We know from contemporary evidence that a cannon had a range of a mile and a half, and a saker had a range of half a mile, so the Walmer guns were effectively covering the Downs anchorage, as intended.

There were eleven trained gunners stationed at Walmer in Elizabeth I's post-Armada time, but presumably the manning was stepped up in times of national emergency. In the time of Charles II, the numbers were much the same.

Deal is preserved just as it was in the time of Henry VIII. It is a masterpiece of sheer uncompromising functionalism, and as such is one of the most fascinating castles in England. Walmer Castle's history has been different. It became the residence of the Warden of the Cinque Ports. It became domesticated. The Duke of Wellington loved Walmer. He called it 'the most charming marine residence I have ever seen. The Queen herself has nothing to compare with it'. In old age, the Duke spent as much time there as he could – and died there.

WESTMINSTER ABBEY

LONDON

Westminster Abbey occupies a unique place in English history; it is both the crowning place and the burial place of most English monarchs.

Westminster began unpromisingly, as a gravel island in the middle of the marshy floodplain of the Thames. The Romans forded the river there, partly because the water was unusually shallow by the Houses of Parliament - and it still is - partly because the gravel island was firm to walk on. The crossing place connected the Dover road (now the A2) to the road to the Midlands (later the A5). The initial link was the ford at Westminster. Later the Romans built a bridge, London Bridge, and then defended it with a fort and a wall; that became Londinium.

By the Saxon period, Londinium had become the thriving and noisy Port of London. The gravel island known as Thorney Island was uninhabited, until, it is said, Sebert King of the East Saxons founded a church on it and had it consecrated by Mellitus, the first Bishop of London, in 616. The first church of which there is any record, though, is the Benedictine abbey dedicated to St Peter in the tenth century.

This was the monastery, the 'West Minster', that Edward the Confessor took over and rebuilt on a grander scale. His Romanesque church was consecrated in 1065. The King died a year later and was buried in it. Miracles were reported almost at once, he was canonized, and the place became a royal pilgrimage focus. In this church, every single monarch since Harold has been crowned, except for Edward V and Edward VIII, who went uncrowned.

Most of the present structure of the abbey is in the Early English style, with the major exceptions of Henry VII's magnificent chapel at the east end, which is in Perpendicular style, and the towers on the west front, which were rebuilt in the eighteenth century. In 1220 a Lady Chapel was added at the east end. In 1245 Henry III decided he would honour Edward the Confessor by rebuilding the entire church in a more magnificent style, and it is that abbey church that we see today. We even know the names of the architects who designed it: Henry de Reyns, John of Gloucester and Robert of Beverley. The height of the nave and the radial arrangement of chapels round the apse are borrowings from French architecture. The magnificent new church was consecrated in 1269.

Westminster Abbey is an architectural masterpiece of the thirteenth to sixteenth centuries. It not only houses the shrine of Edward the Confessor, the tombs of kings and queens, but also many other countless memorials to the famous and the great.

From then on, it became customary for monarchs to be buried in the abbey church. St Edward was buried there, of course, Henry II and Richard I were buried overseas, but from 1269, until George III in 1760 at any rate, all English monarchs were buried in the abbey.

In 1378, Henry Yevele started rebuilding the nave, and the work continued into the time of his successor, but always faithful to the designs drawn up in Henry III's time. The nave vault was not completed until 1506. The new nave was scarcely complete when the Lady Chapel was pulled down to make way for Henry VII's new chapel (finished 1519). Some Norman work still survives in the Chamber of the Pyx and its undercroft.

The exterior has been worked over in the same way. It was also restored by Wren and Wyatt in 1697–1720. The two west towers were designed by Nicholas Hawksmoor in 1735. The facade of the north transept was remodelled by Sir Gilbert Scott in the 1880s. The result of all this is that the outside of the abbey is very unsatisfactory architecturally. The best part of it is the light and delicate walling of Henry VII's Chapel; the rest is too solemn and heavy, with clumsy buttresses that seem to keep the whole building earth-bound.

The interior is far more satisfying. The nave is separated from its side aisles by tall arcades supported on round columns, each of which is surrounded by eight slender shafts of black Purbeck marble. It is the tallest Gothic nave in England, at 31 metres (102 feet), it is half a metre higher than York Minster. Above the arcades is a double triforium with lavish tracery, and above that the tall clerestory.

The nave is full of post-Reformation monuments and memorials to people not buried in the abbey. A few steps in from the west door, in the middle of the nave, is a slab of green marble inscribed 'Remember Winston Churchill'. There is also, immediately to the east, the tomb of the Unknown Soldier, to commemorate the nameless British soldiers who died in the First World War and have unmarked graves elsewhere.

The monuments are a roll of honour of English public life, and include such names as Newton, Congreve, Wordsworth and Darwin. There are too many to list, and there are too many memorials to make a satisfying visual impression. The walls are cluttered with statues, busts, plaques and eulogies, to the point where the place looks more like a flea-market than a great cathedral. Far more satisfactory are the discreet pavement tiles commemorating Elgar, Vaughan Williams and Britten.

The Chapel of Henry VII has superb fan vaulting and graceful

Westminster Abbey has been the setting for every Coronation since 1066 and for numerous other royal occasions. Every monarch since William the Conqueror, with the exception of Edward V and Edward VIII who were never crowned, has been crowned in the Abbey.

On the left is the inside of the Abbey showing the ornate nave windows.

windows. It was begun as a shrine for Henry VI, who was murdered in 1471, and became the burial place of Mary Tudor, Elizabeth I, George II and two children who may have been the Princes in the Tower. The tomb of Henry VII has a very fine effigy of the King by Pietro Torrigiani; James I is buried in the same vault.

The shrine of Edward the Confessor still retains its original stonework in its lower storey, which is thirteenth century; the upper storey is wooden and was added in the sixteenth century. It gives a good idea of what other saints' shrines - including Becket's at Canterbury – must have looked like before they were vandalized by Henry VIII. The tomb of Edward I was opened in 1744; his body, 6ft 2ins tall, was in a good state of preservation and dressed in a gilt crown and royal robes. Nearby is the Coronation Chair, an oak throne made in 1300. Under it, for several centuries, was the Stone of Scone. This was returned to Scotland, for the sake of political correctness, at the close of the twentieth century, though the Scots originally took it from Ireland; it is a royal crowning-stone whose origin is lost in a Celtic twilight.

WINDSOR CASTLE

BERKSHIRE

Windsor is the largest inhabited castle in the world, and the oldest in continuous occupation; English kings and queens have lived there for 900 years.

Windsor Castle, proclaimed by Pepys in the seventeenth century to be 'the most romantique castle that is in the world', had its beginnings a thousand years earlier, when the Saxons settled at Clewer. There may well have been a late Saxon fort on the site of the castle, but the first record we have is of the fort built immediately after the Norman Conquest in 1066. The manor, aptly, belonged to King Harold himself, and he had a palace at Old Windsor; William gave most of the manor away, but kept half a hide bearing an ancient earthwork for himself, and it was here he built his castle, probably in stone from the start; the mound on which the keep stands is a natural chalk hill, and therefore capable of bearing immense weights of stone masonry.

Windsor had obvious strategic significance, overlooking and commanding the middle Thames.

The shell-keep at Windsor is an outstanding building. Following William I's building, the keep was remodelled by Henry II and Edward III and finally reshaped in the nineteenth century. In 1820, it was refaced with new stone and doubled to its present height of 19.5m (64ft). Its walls are a bewildering mix of eleventh, twelfth, fourteenth and nineteenth century stonework.

Windsor quickly became a favourite royal palace, third in rank behind the Tower and Winchester. William II held a council at Windsor, imprisoning the rebel Earl of Mowbray there for the remaining 30 years of his life. Henry II often stayed at Windsor, and had the outer stone curtain wall built in 1175 so that more troops could be garrisoned there.

Henry III did much to improve Windsor. The old hall in the upper ward was abandoned in favour of a new and larger one in the lower ward. In 1272, he roofed the keep. On the town side of the castle, he built three great towers. On the north, he raised another tower on the site now occupied by the Winchester Tower. All the buildings were finely decorated and the windows fitted with glass - a new luxury.

In 1312, Edward III was born at Windsor. During this king's long reign there were many scenes of pomp and ceremony at Windsor, with feasts, processions, tournaments and great assemblies. King Edward was guiding his royal prisoners, King John of France and King David of Scotland, round the lower ward one day when one of them rashly pointed out that the upper ward lay on higher ground and would command a finer view. King Edward agreed and added pleasantly that he would indeed move his castle accordingly and that their two ransoms would pay for the work.

King Edward III was fired by the idea of King Arthur and the Round Table. He wanted to found an order of Knights of the Round Table, and got his carpenters and masons busy with the task of creating a special building to accommodate a round banqueting table. The building was based on the timber lantern at Ely Cathedral; it has completely vanished. The table, made of 52 oaks, seems to have been in the shape of a horseshoe, to allow servants to serve the food and drink. The new order of chivalry became the Order of the Garter.

Prince James of Scotland was held prisoner here for many years. It was while in relaxed captivity that he wrote 'The King's Quair' about his love for the King's niece, Jane Beaufort, whom he eventually married. Ironically, these years were probably the happiest of the young prince's life. When he was released to become King of Scots it was to a gloomy reign culminating in assassination by his own nobles in 1437.

Edward IV was the first English monarch to be buried at Windsor. His treacherous brother, the Duke of Clarence, had been executed in the Tower on Edward's orders, and then buried at Windsor. In 1484, the remains of the murdered Henry VI were transferred from Chertsey Abbey on the orders of Richard III - and buried beside those of his arch-rival, Edward IV. In 1789, some workmen came across the lead coffin of Edward IV. When it was opened, the skeleton was found to be 6ft 4ins tall. A lock of the King's brown hair was taken from the coffin and deposited in the Ashmolean Museum in Oxford.

Queen Elizabeth was very fond of Windsor, sometimes staying there the whole of the autumn

and Christmas. One of the Queen's favourite characters in Shakespeare was Sir John Falstaff, and she expressed a desire to see 'Falstaff in love'; Shakespeare obligingly wrote The Merry Wives of Windsor to please her twice over.

The 1992 fire, on Elizabeth II's wedding anniversary, damaged or destroyed over a hundred rooms. The restoration took five years and £37,000,000 to complete. The disaster prompted searching questions about responsibility for the building and its repair; is Windsor Castle owned by the monarch or the state?

The magnificent St George's Chapel, begun in 1475 by Edward IV and completed by Henry VIII, is one of the finest examples of late medieval architecture in England. Ten monarchs are buried in the chapel, including Henry VIII, who lies with Jane Seymour.

The state apartments are lavishly decorated formal rooms that are still in use for state functions and receptions; they form the centre of a working palace, though they are also open to the public. There is also an outstanding art collection, including works by Leonardo, Rembrandt, Rubens and Van Dyck, and a large collection of armour.

The Norman Gate (above) was built in 1357 as the principal entrance to the Upper Ward of the Castle.

The gloriously souped-up medieval extravaganza that we see today at Windsor is still fundamentally Edward III's castle, but heavily restored. 650 years ago, King Edward spent an incredible £50,000 on Windsor, by far the largest sum any sovereign spent on any single building in the entire middle ages. It was possible only because of Edward's vision, compulsion and sheer ruthlessness. But then, what else is a castle if not a display of brute power?

BATH ABBEY

AVON

Bath Abbey, dedicated to Saint Peter and Saint Paul, was the last of the great pre-Reformation churches to be built. The abbey stands in the centre of the town, close to the Roman Baths and the Pump Room. It has a conventional cross-shaped plan, with a tower 50m (162ft) tall at the crossing. The tower is unusual, in having a rectangular plan rather than the usual square; this is because the transepts are quite narrow and the nave and choir are wide.

The most outstanding feature of Bath Abbey is undoubtedly its west front, which has a magnificent window. On each side are turrets with ladders to Heaven carved on them, with angels passing up and down.

The site has a long and remarkable history, beginning as an iron age religious site, with hot springs as the focus of a major pagan sanctuary. The springs in the marsh were the haunt of a local goddess called Sul. During the Roman occupation, this was taken over and developed by the Romans, who called the place Aquae Sulis. Sul herself was taken over and equated with the Roman goddess Minerva. When the Romans left, the place was called Badon, and Arthur's first great battle was probably fought on the valley side to the east of the town. The Saxons took it over in 577 and renamed it Hat Bathu (At the Baths). In 676, a local Christian king called Osric endowed a religious house which was both a monastery and a nunnery.

By the tenth century, Bath had become such an important focus that Edgar was crowned King of England there in 973. A hundred years later, under Norman rule, work was begun on a cathedral, on the site of the present abbey. Very little of the Norman church, built by Bishop John de Villula, has survived other than a single arch in the south-east corner of the abbey church. This arch led from the south transept into the Norman south aisle of the nave.

Bishop John de Villula decided to transfer the seat of his bishopric from Wells to Bath, which led to a long and bitter rivalry between the two towns. In the thirteenth century the Pope confirmed the title 'Bishop of Bath and Wells'. The dispute between the two towns only ended in 1539, when Bath Abbey was dissolved and Wells became the only bishopric in Somerset; the bishops nevertheless continued to use the double title.

When de Villula died in 1122 Bath Abbey entered a period of decline. The building was occasionally patched, but unsatisfactorily. Thus it was that in 1499 Bishop Oliver King began work on a completely new church, on the same site, but much smaller than the old one. The entire length of the present building fits onto the site of the Norman nave, making it about half the length of its predecessor. Bishop King had a vision of angels, which inspired him to build the church, and which is commemorated in the carvings on the west front. King was a friend of the secular King, Henry VII, who lent him his master masons, the brothers William and Robert Vertue.

The Dissolution inevitably delayed the completion of the building, and it was not consecrated until 1616. The interior of the abbey was restored by Sir Gilbert Scott in the 1860s.

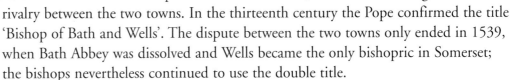

Because of the many beautiful windows inside Bath Abbey, it is known locally as the 'Lantern of the West'. The Abbey is also noted for the superb fan vaulting with its scalloped effect.

CORFE CASTLE

DORSET

Corfe Castle is a dramatic ruin in a dramatic setting, standing on a steep-sided, natural conical hill commanding the narrow, ravine-like gap through the chalk ridge that defends the Isle of Purbeck. The gap was once called 'Corvesgate'. On each side, to north and south, are expanses of desolate heathland. The castle stands in the narrow gap like a soldier in a sentry box – very much on guard duty.

There was a castle here at least as early as the tenth century, well before the Norman conquest. It was rebuilt by the Normans, modernized and completed in the thirteenth century after being re-created in stone in the reigns of King John and Edward I. Then, and for four centuries after, Corfe Castle must have been one of the most imposing fortresses in England. It was totally impregnable until weapon technology enabled fire power to reach it from the hills to east and west.

The Norman castle builders used the same local Purbeck limestone that was used to build the village that grew up beside the castle, a village of quarrymen and stone carvers. Through that busy village of quarrymen and master masons passed armed troops on their way to and from the castle, and also kings and queens and their retinues.

Corfe Castle was the scene of an historic assassination, the murder of the Saxon King Edward the Martyr. In 978, the castle probably consisted of no more than a few domestic buildings within an inner ward of stone, surrounded by a timber palisade. There was a gatehouse on the south side, giving access to the castle from the village. The boy-king was arriving at the gatehouse, when he was stabbed to death while being greeted by his step-mother. It was she who master-minded the murder. Fatally stabbed, the youth tried to ride away, but fainted and fell from his horse. His foot caught in the stirrup and he was dragged along by his horse. Miracles were claimed, and the dead king was proclaimed a saint and martyr.

The castle was rebuilt at William the Conqueror's orders, and in 1100 it was fitted with a large keep and a large outer bailey built of stone, giving it something close to its appearance today. The keep was a bleak, austere, thick-walled cube 21m (70ft) high. It was reached by a path that wound up the slope, passing through one defence after another. The already strong fortress was further strengthened by King John; he wanted to use it as a state prison and a strong-room for the crown jewels. The Butavant or Dungeon Tower was raised at the western edge of the west bailey, where very steep slopes made a natural defence. Among King John's prisoners here were twenty-two French aristocrats. John ordered that they should be given neither food nor water. Their deaths added another crime to the list of dark deeds committed at Corfe Castle. King John murdered his nephew Duke Arthur of Brittany with his own hands, then imprisoned Arthur's sister Eleanor at Corfe for many years before moving her on to Bristol, where she died after spending most of her life in pointless captivity.

John extended the curtain walls and strengthened the existing buildings at Corfe. He also built the Gloriette range round a courtyard; this was evidently an important addition, though what its use was is not clear.

Henry III had the chapel built and ordered the whole castle to be whitewashed. It made good practical sense to whitewash the interior, because the windows were very small and it was the only way to make the chambers light. Sometimes the exteriors of castles were also painted white, perhaps to make them more conspicuous, perhaps to cover up variations in the quality of masonry and possible weak points.

Corfe later became a prison for another distinguished royal prisoner, the deposed Edward II, who was kept there for a while before being taken to Berkeley Castle, where it is generally believed he was murdered. The King's brother, the Earl of Kent, did not believe he had been murdered at all, but still languished in the dungeons at Corfe. The Constable of Corfe Castle encouraged him to think this. The Earl sent messages to his (probably) dead brother via the constable, but the constable delivered them to Queen Isabella and Roger Mortimer, and they arranged for the Earl too to vanish.

Corfe Castle is one of the most evocative ruined castles in England and has over 1,000 years of turbulent history. There is the belief that it may have been a Roman defensive site, but the remains of the castle we see today were a rebuild in the eleventh century of what was a wood castle back into the ninth century.

Eventually Elizabeth I inherited Corfe Castle, and she gave it to one her favourites, Sir Christopher Hatton. In the seventeenth century, it passed into the ownership of Sir John Bankes, the Attorney General. In 1643, when Sir John Bankes was away, the castle was surrounded by a Parliamentarian army and Lady Bankes had to defend it herself. This she did very successfully for three years. In the end it was a royalist island in a huge region occupied by Parliamentarian troops. It was only taken when one of the defending officers, Colonel Pitman, betrayed Lady Bankes by letting the Parliamentary soldiers in.

Parliament immediately ordered the slighting of Corfe Castle. The foundations of the castle's defences were quarried away and the buildings were blown up with gunpowder. Some walls collapsed down the hillside. Some towers tilted out of the perpendicular. The south tower of the gatehouse, sometimes called Edward the Martyr's Gate, was broken away from its foundations and blown sideways, so that it now stands, upright and intact, some metres from its original position. This is one of the visitors' first sights of the castle, approaching the gatehouse from the picturesque village.

The slighting was so thorough and so effective that the castle was not only indefensible but uninhabitable. It was never again lived in after 1646.

Instead, Corfe Castle became – in the space of a few days – the archetypal ruined castle, the ultimate Gothic folly. Although it arrived at its ruinous state suddenly and all at once, it somehow epitomizes in people's minds the distance between the present day and England's historic past. As a result, it attracts many more visitors than castles that remain intact.

Corfe Castle was the inspiration for 'Kirrin Castle' in some of Enid Blyton's stories, and Brownsea Island for 'Whispering Island'.

GLASTONBURY ABBEY

SOMERSET

Glastonbury Abbey is still a noble and inspiring sight, though it is only a fragment of what originally stood on this unusual spot, a hill rising sharply out of the Somerset Levels. When the abbey was dissolved in 1539, it was unroofed and the walls left open to the weather. The shell of the great abbey then served as a quarry for building stone; much of the town of Glastonbury was built out of blocks scavenged from the huge church and its ancillary buildings.

None of the visible walls is older than 1184. There was an abbey on the site before, but there was a devastating fire on 24 May 1184 that necessitated a total rebuild. Only one chamber and the bell tower were left standing of the magnificent monastery with its abbey church that had been the resting place of many saints.

The story of that older abbey was long and distinguished, and it was assembled by one of the leading medieval historians, William of Malmesbury. At the invitation of the Glastonbury monks, William wrote a book on Glastonbury's history. Unfortunately, William was a guest at the abbey and felt an obligation to please his hosts, so the story was inflated with some incredible legends. William begins the story with King Lucius, a legendary British ruler who is supposed to have lived in the second century. Lucius travelled to Rome, where Pope Eleutherius supplied him with missionaries. Lucius returned, converted the people and founded the Church of St Mary at Glastonbury. This story had for a long time been 'authorized' by Bede, but William also quoted another foundation legend, in which the monks audaciously attributed the founding of Glastonbury to the disciples of Christ. William evidently did not believe this, writing that he would 'leave disputable matters'. William of Malmesbury significantly says nothing about some of the more controversial legends which were presumably invented by the Glastonbury monks after William had written his history.

The site of Glastonbury is a hilly peninsula, a finger of land pointing out into the marshes. On the neck of the peninsula is a massive earthwork, Ponter's Ball, raised in the late iron age. This suggests that Glastonbury was an important pagan sanctuary. Holy precincts at that time were often associated with hills beside springs – Giant Hill at Cerne Abbas springs to mind - and Glastonbury shares this association. The main spring on the island, Chalice Well, lies immediately below the summit, Glastonbury Tor. The existence of a great pagan sanctuary on the Isle of Glastonbury would explain the interest shown in the site by Christian missionaries. Pope Gregory instructed specifically that Christian missionaries should take over pagan sanctuaries and then win the pagans round gradually to Christian rites.

The core and centre of the new Christian monastery was the ancient cemetery round the Lady Chapel, which was built on the site of the older Church of St Mary. Within and beside this cemetery were small oratories built of wattle and daub. It was in this ancient cemetery

that the monks perpetrated their most shameless fraud; they claimed that they found the bodies of King Arthur and his queen there. William of Malmesbury made no mention of this tradition in 1120, so it presumably did not exist then. By 1191, the monks were digging up the royal log coffins and ceremonially transferring the remains of Arthur and Guinevere to a shrine in the choir of the abbey church.

The Great Church, as it was later described, was begun late in the twelfth century and enough of it was finished for the monks to take possession at Christmas 1213. It consisted of a choir of seven bays for the monks, with two side aisles, a very long nave of nine bays, also with two side aisles, two massive transepts and a spacious crossing under a soaring central tower. At the eastern end of this colossus there was an additional chapel, called the Edgar Chapel, which was built on later. At the western end there was the final addition, a spacious porch called the Galilee, built in the fourteenth century, which linked the new church building with the old Lady Chapel, making it an amazing 161m (530ft) long overall.

The Great Church was one of the finest religious buildings ever to be built in England - indeed, one of the very finest buildings of any kind. The loss of this architectural masterpiece is one of the scandals of Henry VIII's reign. To the south of this endless church was a large cloister, a chapter house, a refectory, a kitchen and a dormitory. Separate, and to the south-west were the Abbot's Hall and kitchen. To the north of that lay the site of the ancient cemetery, now levelled up to make a pleasant garden.

The Great Church needed to be a splendid and spectacular building. It needed to attract pilgrims. Pilgrims were the basis of the tourist industry of the middle ages. To attract pilgrims, a sacred site had to look and feel very special. Here we have the motive for the monks' fabrication of the Arthur and Guinevere graves. The legends gave the Glastonbury experience a special edge over other pilgrimage centres – and there were many competitors. The Great Church itself was a spectacular focus that pulled the pilgrims (and their money) in from all over England and mainland Europe. Like Canterbury and Santiago de Compostela, Glastonbury was one of the major pilgrimage centres of Europe.

The enormous wealth of Glastonbury caught Henry VIII's greedy eye. His commissioners reported that 'the house is greate, goodly, and so pryncely as we have not sene the lyke.' The abbot, who lived like a duke, was a man of 80 and not about to change his ways. Richard Whiting refused to surrender his abbey. Worse, he hid the abbey's plate to stop the king getting hold of it. The elderly abbot was arrested, charged with treason and tried, though the trial was a sham. Cromwell noted beforehand, 'Item: the Abbot of Glaston to be tried at Glaston, and also be executed there.' On 15 November 1539, the white-haired abbot was dragged on a hurdle to the summit of Glastonbury Tor, where he was hanged, drawn and quartered. His head was stuck on a pole over the abbey gate. It was by any standards a terrible thing Cromwell had done in Henry VIII's name. And then the abbey itself underwent its martyrdom, its stones torn out for shops and houses and to pave the road to Wells.

The mysterious Glastonbury Tor (right). There are many myths and legends associated with the Tor - it is the home of Gwyn ap Nudd, the Lord of the Underworld and King of the Fairies, and a place where the fairy folk live. In early-medieval times there was a small monks' retreat on top of the Tor, founded probably in the time of St Patrick in the mid-400s. This was followed in the early 1100s by a chapel, St Michael de Torre. This was destroyed in a powerful earthquake in 1275 and rebuilt in the early 1300s. The tower is all that remains today.

NUNNEY CASTLE

SOMERSET

Nunney Castle sits placidly in the middle of Nunney village, three miles south-west of Frome, and is as far from being an oppressive and forbidding seat of military power as could be imagined. It was in fact never intended to be a real fortress, but a high-status mansion, and must have been something of a picturesque folly even when it was built. The big, drum-shaped angle-towers give an impression of solidity and strength, but close examination reveals that they are built of rather small stones; this is not at all the sort of masonry that was needed to withstand a cannon ball or a battering ram.

Nunney is a four-storey tower-house, and it was built in 1373 by Sir John de la Mare (or Delamere), using the proceeds of his fighting in the Hundred Years War. The rectangular tower or keep has cylindrical towers projecting from its corners and the building as a whole is surrounded by a moat. The central feature is a courtyard. There were other such courtyard castles, such as Chillingham in Northumberland and Amberley in Sussex. Sometimes the corner towers were built so close together that the courtyard was virtually squeezed out and all that is left is a light well – and that is what happened at Nunney. This was the practice at some French castles, and it looks as if Sir John brought back the idea for Nunney's design from his French campaigning, along with the money to pay for it. Sir John de la Mare was not alone in this, either. Another veteran of the French wars, John, fifth Lord Lovell, built Old Wardour Castle not far away in Wiltshire on the model of a specific French castle, the Chateau de Concressault. Both Nunney and Old Wardour are strongly French-influenced examples of 'collapsed courtyard' castles.

It is like a cut-price version of Bodiam, a beautiful miniature castle. This arrangement was originally set in a bailey surrounded by a curtain wall on three sides and a stream on the fourth, but these defences would not have kept Nunney safe from even a casual attack.

Sir John was really dressing up his luxury home a little and

Nunney Castle is more of a fortified manor house than a castle, which was doubtless its real purpose, as it was quite useless as a fortress. It had a moat with a bridge over it but no sign of a drawbridge or portcullis. Its towers do not have battlements and it seems that originally they were topped with conical roofs in typical French style. Nunney did not have a commanding position as a castle should have, but was set on low terrain compared with nearby ground and therefore cannot be seen except from its immediate surroundings.

wanted the status of being a castle-dwelling war veteran, but he was evidently not expecting any serious trouble. Nor was there any. The date of the licence to crenellate, 1373, does not coincide with any invasion scare. The de la Mares handed their castle on intact to the Paulets and the Praters. A small but dangerous resistance was made on the King's behalf in the Civil War, though, and for that it was slighted by Cromwell's men. The north side of the castle was so weakened by the seventeenth century slighting that as recently as 1910 it fell down to expose the interior, rather like a doll's house with the front swung open. Inside, it is possible to see the chambers, garderobes and spiral stairs of a comfortable medieval manor house.

In Nunney Castle, we can share an elderly medieval knight's nostalgia for military glory, and dream the old campaigner's dream of knightly chivalry.

OLD WARDOUR CASTLE

WILTSHIRE

Old Wardour Castle, between Shaftesbury and Wilton, and near Donhead St Andrews, lies buried in the depths of rural Wiltshire. It was built in the late fourteenth century by the Lovell family. The castle or rather keep stands in the middle of a bailey surrounded by a curtain wall, but it is clear even from the most cursory glance that this was a mansion rather than a fortress.

The original fortified house was raised in 1393, when Sir John Lovell was granted a licence to crenellate. It was built round a small six-sided courtyard, with large square towers at the corners. Lovell was a veteran of the French wars and he modelled his castle on a French courtyard castle.

Old Wardour Castle was modernized in the sixteenth century after Sir Matthew Arundell bought the castle. Most of the architectural details on the house belong to that 'restoration' phase. The Arundells were staunch Catholics, and Matthew's son Thomas was created a Count of the Holy Roman Empire before James I made him an English baron.

The Arundells were also Royalists, so in 1646 the 25 defenders of Old Wardour Castle found themselves besieged by a thousand Parliamentarian soldiers. The defence was led by Lady Blanche Arundell. The Parliamentarian troops began undermining the walls, so Lady Blanche surrendered. After the women and children had been led away into captivity, the soldiers wantonly damaged the house and grounds.

The following year, it was the Royalists' turn to lay siege to Old Wardour, this time to shift the Parliamentarians who were garrisoned there. The Parliamentarians resisted for longer than was expected, thanks to the inspiring leadership of Robert Balsom. The Royalists had meanwhile done a lot of damage to the house as they tried to restore it to Lord Arundell. The castle was mined – by Lord Arundell himself – to make sure no-one else got his castle. John Aubrey saw the ruin the day after the explosion, and was surprised that one little tower which was partially knocked over was still held together by its mortar.

The Arundell family built a new mansion nearby, but did not demolish the old one. The ruin stands as a monument to the Hundred Years War and to the prevailing madness of war in general. Here is a castle blown up by its owner.

The grounds of the ruins were landscaped in romantic style, with a grotto made of stone, plaster and brick. The elaborate Tudor alterations are still visible. The compact 'French-influenced' plan was kept by the Arundells. The ruin had to have vegetation sprouting from every cranny to be a true romantic ruin, though much of this has been removed. The architect Robert Smythson designed a lot of the new detail, including the magnificent entrance to the great hall from the courtyard, with Tuscan columns and lions' heads. Lady Blanche is still, they say, to be seen on the walls, loading the defenders' guns. Lady Blanche did everything she could to defend her family's castle, yet she later had to watch as her husband deliberately blew the castle up as a point of principle.

Despite its ruinous state today, it is apparent that no expense was spared in building this splendid castle. The high quality workmanship and excellent masonry, using locally quarried Tisbury greensand, are still very much in evidence.

ST MICHAEL'S MOUNT

CORNWALL

St Michael's Mount is a granite crag rising startlingly out of the sea in the middle of St Michael's Bay, accessible on foot only at low tide across a causeway. It is a superb site for a castle, but it has had a very mixed use. The little rocky island's long history began with the coastwise trade in stone axes during the neolithic age, and it went on to become a major port in the iron age.

The Mount has also found its way into several strands of British legend, including the stories of Tristan and Isolde and Jack the Giant Killer. The giant Cormoran, who lived on it, used to wade ashore and snatch cows to eat. Jack is alleged to have killed Cormoran by blowing on his horn and getting the giant to run down the hillside into a pit. The pit or well, now sealed, is still visible.

Diodorus Siculus described how St Michael's Mount became a major trading post in the iron age. 'They convey [Cornish tin] to an island which lies off Britain and is called Ictis; for at the ebb-tide the space between this island and the mainland becomes dry and they can take the tin in large quantities over to the islands on their wagons. On the island of Ictis, the [Greek] merchants purchase the tin from the natives and carry it to Galatia or Gaul'.

The island's dedication dates from AD 495, when a group of fishermen standing on a ledge high on the island's western side had a vision of St Michael.

After the Norman Conquest, much of the West Country was given to Robert Count of Mortain, who became Earl of Cornwall. Robert in turn granted the Mount to the Norman Abbey of Mont St Michel; a priory was established there in 1135 by Bernard of Le Bec. The site nevertheless made it ideal for a fortress. In the twelfth century it was seized and held as a fortress by some of Prince John's supporters while Richard I was away. Afterwards the rock returned to its monastic use, but it was seized by Henry V during the war with France, and by 1424 all links between the Mount and its French counterpart were severed. The Mount was once more used as a fortress in the Wars of the Roses and the Cornish Rebellion against Edward VI.

The last time St Michael's Mount was used as a fortress was in 1646, during the Civil War. It was held for a while by Royalist supporters, but they were obliged to surrender to Parliamentarian troops. The Mount was bought by the last military governor of the Mount, Sir John St Aubyn, in 1660 and since then has led an uninterrupted peaceful existence. For many years the house was used by the St Aubyns as a second home, mainly during the summer, but during the eighteenth century they established it as their principal home, adding a large new wing with impressive Victorian apartments. The St Aubyn family owned St Michael's Mount until 1964, when it was handed over to the National Trust.

CASTLE ACRE CASTLE & PRIORY

NORFOLK

The priory at Castle Acre has withstood the ravages of time and tyrant better than the castle. The priory is the most important Cluniac ruin in England; the only other to come anywhere near rivalling it is Wenlock in Shropshire. It is also the most impressive ruin of any kind in East Anglia.

The castle was probably built by William de Warenne, the same Warenne who built the castle at Lewes, and who introduced the Cluniac order into England. There is a story that Gundrada, Warenne's wife, died at Castle Acre, but this seems unlikely as it is known that she was buried at Lewes Priory.

The architecture at the Cluniac priory was lavish by comparison with the austere Cistercian houses; the Cluniacs were more renowned for their elaborate church services than for more practical matters like sheep-rearing. The west front of the priory stands almost to its full height. Its Norman doorway, with four orders of columns and intricate mouldings, is flanked by smaller doorways. The stone is brown sandstone, and the carving is the work of a mason called Ulmar; he had been 'donated' to the priory by the lord of the manor. Over the main door a big Gothic window was inserted in the fifteenth century.

Behind this impressive facade, little remains except fragments. There was an aisled nave and a central tower that stood on four massive stone-encased piers. What we see today are weathered remnants of broken arches and soaring towers of flint, the main local building material. The ruins look like a collection of sea-stacks shattered by Atlantic waves. Covering 14.6 hectares (36 acres), it is hard to believe that they served only 26 monks.

During Edward I's reign, Castle Acre Priory was fortified against Benedict, who had been appointed prior in place of the 'sitting tenant', William of Shoreham. The retainers of the lord of the manor came to William's aid, and saw off the intruder.

The priory attracted large numbers of pilgrims, who came to see 'divers relics of saints'. One of these was the arm of St Philip.

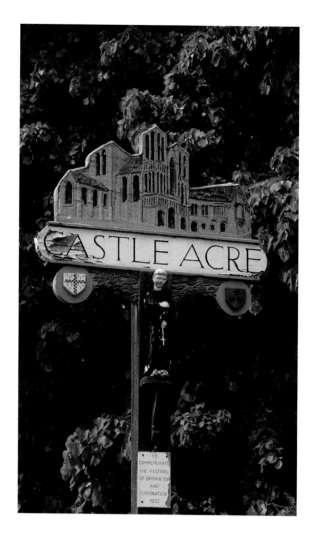

The village sign seen on the Castle Acre village green shows a monk and the cluniac Priory which stands on the west side of this Norfolk village.

In 1537, the priory was dissolved and the buildings became a stone quarry for all the builders in the area. Much of the ashlared facing stone was taken, leaving only the flint rubble cores of the walls. The site has been left looking utterly ravaged. The land passed through the hands of the Duke of Norfolk, and then after his disgrace and execution into those of Thomas Gresham, one of Elizabeth I's favourites. The Cecils became owners and finally the Coke family. While the Cokes owned the site, parts of the west range, which had once been the prior's lodging, were turned into a dwelling house.

The ruins of Castle Acre Priory stand at the edge of Castle Acre village, which lies within the huge outer bailey of the castle. The whole site, some four miles north of Swaffham, lies on the even more ancient course of the Peddars Way, an old road that was used by pilgrims in the middle ages, by Roman soldiers, and by the native people back in the iron age too. The castle and priory are so badly wrecked that it is very hard to visualize what they looked like in their hey-day – but they were certainly large and impressive buildings.

The picture above shows the remains of Castle Acre Priory as it can be seen today, and below the Castle and Priory together.

CASTLE RISING

Two mysterious royal deaths are linked with Castle Rising. The first is the death of Henry I in 1135. He was said by contemporaries to have died 'of a surfeit of lampreys' – probably food poisoning. His widow, Queen Adelaide of Louvain, remarried two years later. Her new husband was William d'Albini, the Earl of Arundel, and he built a fine castle at Castle Rising to mark his promoted status as consort of the Queen of England.

Castle Rising is a backwater now, but then it was a place of consequence. A local verse has it that –

Rising was a seaport when Lynn was but a marsh.

Now Lynn it is a seaport town and Rising fares the worse.

The wheel of fortune was turned about by the recession of the sea, which left the old port stranded.

The fine old castle rises from massive earthworks. It is thought that the earthworks may be Roman in origin. There is a very deep ditch with a high rampart on the inner side, and this surrounds a circular bailey. In the bailey, squats a great square unroofed keep.

The keep is an exceptionally fine piece of Norman architecture showing a refined taste, with a great deal of ornamental stonework on the outside – very unusual for a keep. Perhaps William wanted his keep to delight the eye of his new bride. There were several rooms on each of the original two floors, and the entrance was at first floor level, reached by an external stone staircase.

In the fourteenth century, Castle Rising became the property of Edward III, who installed his mother Isabella there after the execution of her lover, Roger Mortimer. This is where the second mysterious royal death enters Castle Rising's story: the horrible murder at Berkeley Castle of Edward II. The names of the assassins are known, but there is no proof that they were acting on direct orders from Edward's wife, Isabella, or her lover, Mortimer. The circumstantial evidence is overwhelming, though, and most people at the time and subsequently have assumed that she was guilty.

Given his mother's evident connivance at the cruel murder of his father, Edward II, Edward III can hardly have known what to do with her. The only option seemed to be to keep her well out of the way. The dowager queen, known as 'the She-wolf of France', was kept under house-arrest at Castle Rising, where she was regularly visited by Edward III, though whether out of affection, filial duty or suspicion is not clear. Another visitor was the Black Prince, who later became the castle's owner.

In those days, the keep did not stand on its own in the bailey, but was surrounded by other ancillary buildings. The castle would have looked – and functioned – like a miniature medieval town. There were granaries, stables, a chapel and lodgings. All of these buildings have gone. There is now but a fragment of the Norman gatehouse still standing near the tower.

By the reign of Edward IV, Castle Rising was said to have 'no room in it but let in rain, wind and snow'.

In 1572 a survey was made of Castle Rising and the following description was given to Queen Elizabeth I, that it was:

'Erected at the first but for the speare and shield, and for that force it may be maynteynde if it please her Majestie to be at the charge. This charge they estimate at £2000. And further, if the same castle should be taken downe and sold for benefitt, it is so greatlie decaied as the same will not yeald above one hundred markes' (£66.67)

ELY CATHEDRAL

CAMBRIDGESHIRE

The name 'Ely' means 'Eel Island', and the tiny city stands on a low, dry island of gravel about 21m (70 feet) above the reclaimed marshland. Although 21m is not high, it is high enough to make the huge cathedral very conspicuous in the vast plain of the Fens.

The city of Ely may be tiny, but its cathedral is huge. At 158m (517ft), it is one of the longest churches in England. It is also one of the most varied architecturally.

The first building at Ely was a Benedictine abbey for monks and nuns, founded by St Etheldreda, Queen of Northumbria. She settled at this secluded island in the Fens when she retired from the world in 673 to become Ely's first abbess. After her death in 679 miracles were reported by those praying at her shrine, and Ely became a major focus for Saxon pilgrims.

In 870 the Danes sacked the abbey, but it was refounded a few decades later by King Edgar (959–75) as a Benedictine monastery. Following the Norman invasion, Ely was used as a headquarters by the Saxon resistance led by Hereward the Wake in 1070–71.

William I appointed a fellow Norman, Simeon, as abbot, and Simeon began work on the present structure in 1083. The Norman transepts and east end were finished in 1106. In 1109 the church was raised to cathedral status, though the Norman nave was not completed until 1189. The nave is narrow, almost 76m (250ft) long and made up of 12 bays. It is an imposing piece of Late Norman architecture, virtually contemporary with the nave of Peterborough cathedral. The piers are fairly massive, as Norman pillars usually are, but lighter than those of Durham or Gloucester. The original plain roof has been replaced by a nineteenth century ceiling, which some people may like.

In the south aisle of the nave is the Prior's Doorway, which was built in about 1140. This is normally kept locked in winter, but on the outside it has a richly carved tympanum, the semicircular panel contained between the door lintel and the arch. This tympanum shows Christ in majesty, and such compositions are sometimes just called 'Majesties'. The pilasters are also carved, with figures of beasts and men. Close to this door is the plinth of a Saxon cross, which is called Ovin's Stone. It was dedicated to Ovinus, a leading Anglo-Saxon in the time of Queen Etheldreda.

Near the west end of the nave is the grave of Alan de Walsingham, the architect of the Octagon. His brass has unfortunately gone.

The transepts are large. They are also unusual in having aisles, just like miniature naves. The lower walls of the transepts have some of the oldest surviving

masonry in the cathedral, dating from as early as 1083.

The choir contains the tomb of John Tiptoft, Earl of Worcester, between his two wives; he was beheaded in 1470 during the Wars of the Roses. In front of the high altar there is an inscribed slate slab marking the site of the shrine of St Etheldreda.

The Galilee, or west porch, was added in about 1200. Bishop Hugh of Northwold lengthened the choir by six graceful bays in the new Early English style, and these were to be the setting for St Etheldreda's shrine.

In 1322, disaster struck. The central tower fell down, wrecking the Norman nave. This gave the sacrist Alan de Walsingham and his team of craftsmen an opportunity to try something new. They designed the beautiful and entirely original octagonal lantern above the crossing – a much lighter and therefore safer structure than the Norman stone tower.

The chantry chapels at the east end of the church were built later in the Perpendicular style, between 1490 and 1520. The unsatisfactory and asymmetrical appearance of the west front is simply explained by the collapse of the north-west tower in 1701. The west front is full of interest, but badly needs restoration to its original symmetry.

Ultimately, it is the unique central Octagon that is the cathedral's main interest – and one of the marvels of medieval architecture. The timber lantern was restored by Sir George Gilbert Scott in the nineteenth century. When viewed from below, the interlaced timberwork is as fascinating to look at as the stone tracery of a decorated window. Aesthetically the Octagon works well, supplying an oasis of light and airy space in the midst of some rather heavy and oppressive Norman stonework. It has been compared to a huge starfish, with the light-filled space of the lantern as the body and the vaulting that spreads the weight out to the supporting columns as the arms. The wooden lantern weighs 400 tons, and the engineers had to search far and wide throughout England to find oaks big enough for the corner posts, which are 19m (63ft) long. The master carpenter employed by Alan de Walsingham was William Hurley, the most famous carpenter of his day.

High up on the arches of the Octagon are carved stone heads, including portraits of Edward III, Queen Philippa, Alan de Walsingham, Prior Crauden and Bishop Hotham, though these can only be appreciated with binoculars. A tour round the outside of Ely Cathedral offers a constantly changing kaleidoscope of shapes and surfaces, from the bluff straightforwardness of the Norman work to the ornate and fancy work of the Octagon. The octagonal top storey of the tower is decorated in style, but the lower part belongs to the late Norman period.

The west front is odd. Normally west fronts have a flanking tower on each side. Ely was designed to have flanking towers, but the north-west tower fell down in a storm in 1701 and was never rebuilt. The effect of the complete design could be impressive, but the continuing lopsidedness is entirely unsatisfactory.

From a distance, Ely Cathedral looks far less appealing, rising forbiddingly from the flat Fens like a beached oil tanker.

One of the most outstanding features of Ely Cathedral is the stone work of the Octagon. William Hurley, Edward III's master carpenter devised Ely's famous lantern tower. It took 14 years to build, but still stands today, a masterpiece of medieval engineering. It weighs 200 tons of timber, lead and glass.

FRAMLINGHAM CASTLE

SUFFOLK

Framlingham is one of the most beautiful medieval castles in Britain. The site was probably fortified in the Saxon period. An early Norman timber castle was raised there in the eleventh century. Roger Bigod is the first known owner of the castle, and he was granted Framlingham in 1101 by Henry I.

Roger Bigod died in 1107 and his son and heir died in the famous 'White Ship' disaster along with William Audelin in 1120. Roger's second son, Hugh, inherited Framlingham and became Earl of Norfolk. Hugh probably built a motte type of castle at Framlingham in about 1140.

When Henry II came to the English throne, Hugh was confirmed as owner of Framlingham; he had helped Henry to the throne and this was his reward. But then Hugh quarrelled with Henry II and in retaliation the king confiscated Framlingham. In 1165, Hugh raised enough money to buy his castle back, but the king took the precaution of having Orford Castle built close by in order to maintain control over Hugh. Hugh was implicated in the barons' revolt in 1173, the castle was once again confiscated – and this time completely destroyed.

When Richard I came to the throne, Hugh was dead and his son Roger, the second Earl of Norfolk, was in favour with the king. In this way, the family regained ownership of Framlingham. It was Roger who built the castle as we now see it, with its splendid polygonal curtain wall laced with thirteen graceful towers. It was a revolutionary design that enabled a large force of infantry and cavalry to be housed and protected. The new castle reflected crusader experience, and contained memories of the walls and towers at Constantinople. In some ways, Framlingham's design looked ahead to Caernarvon.

Framlingham Castle changed hands a number of times, passing through the hands of the Dukes of Norfolk, who made it their chief residence in the fifteenth century. The first Howard Duke of Norfolk was killed at Bosworth in 1485. His son, the second Duke, was pardoned by Henry VII and became the victor at Flodden. He modernized the castle, using brick extensively, adding the fine bridge and gatehouse, and topping the towers with a set of magnificent Tudor chimneys – and all of them except one are purely for decorative effect.

Unusually, Framlingham does not have a keep. A larger outer bailey formerly existed to the east and south and in the sixteenth century

All that is left of Framlingham Castle is the curtain wall. The crenellations on the top of the wall acted as protection for the guards, who stood behind them to fire arrows out of the arrow slits (shown above).

enclosed most of the town. It was huge, and could house an entire army.

In old age Henry VIII imprisoned the third duke and confiscated Framlingham, and after his death Edward VI gave it to his half-sister, Mary Tudor. For a moment Framlingham stood at the centre of British history. It was at Framlingham that Mary waited with her army, to see whether she was to succeed to the throne. When her brother, the boy-king Edward VI, died in 1553, she was challenged by the Duke of Northumberland, who raised an army in support of his daughter-in-law, Lady Jane Grey. Mary retreated to her great castle at Framlingham – where she was safe – before marching forth to take her throne.

Although a traditional keep was not built within the castle, Framlingham does have a very impressive series of thirteen towers set along the length of a magnificent curtain wall that looks today almost as it would have 800 years ago. However, inside, almost nothing remains of the original castle save for a few traces of fireplaces, and the seventeenth century almshouse building.

HEDINGHAM CASTLE

ESSEX

Hedingham Castle is dominated by its great four-storey square keep. It is not a site of great beauty, but it does nevertheless boast what is considered to be one of the best surviving – and best-preserved – examples of Norman military towers.

The keep was built in about 1130 by Aubrey de Vere, within a bailey surrounded by a moat. It is a very imposing and oppressive piece of architecture. It is unusually tall. Many Norman keeps were built 18–19m (60–65ft) high. This one stood over 30m (100ft) high when complete, with walls twelve feet thick at the base. The walls are of rubble faced with neatly coursed Barnack stone, most of which is still in place.

There was an annexe on the west side of the keep, which may have functioned as a prison, but this is badly ruined. The entrance to the keep was on this side, by way of an exterior staircase to a door at first floor level, a common defensive device. The doorway has a fine carved Romanesque arch with zig-zag ornament and round attached columns on each side. Inside, there was a spiral staircase rising to the battlements, where the four angle turrets and a protective parapet rose above roof level. The staircase, as is usual in castles, was mounted in a clockwise direction. This enabled retreating (or advancing) defenders to use their sword arms effectively, but gave little room for the attackers to swing their swords; the newel post got in the way.

The keep at Hedingham Castle was fitted with wall fireplaces, and was one of the earliest English castles to have chimney flues built into the walls – a feature shortly to become universal in both castle and domestic architecture. The de Vere family were clearly interested in domestic comfort as well as military strength. The hall on the second floor was a splendid chamber, with a gallery all the way round it and a huge round arch – the widest Norman arch in the whole of England – supporting the lofty ceiling.

It is said that King Stephen's wife, Matilda of Boulogne, died at Hedingham Castle in 1152. In the reign of King John the de Veres sided with the barons against the King, and their castle was captured by him. Later family members supported the House of Lancaster in the Wars of the Roses, and died as a result. These sacrifices might have been rewarded by the Tudor monarchs, but the Tudors were short on gratitude. When John de Vere entertained Henry VII here, he went to a lot of expense, and assembled a large retinue of retainers in his Oxford livery. His Majesty was daunted by what he evidently saw as a show of strength, and on his departure he chillingly pointed out that de Vere had broken a recent law forbidding this practice. The King fined him 15,000 marks.

The ruinous state of Hedingham today is, unusually, not due to the Civil War but to the folly of one of its owners, the seventeenth Earl of Oxford. He was a poor manager, a spendthrift and a drunkard. He dismantled the property at the end of the sixteenth century and left it in its current state.

There are four floors to explore at Hedingham Castle, including a magnificent Banqueting Hall spanned by a remarkable 28 foot arch, one of the largest Norman arches in England. A good view of this splendid room can be obtained from the Minstrels' Gallery, built within the thickness of the 12 foot walls.

NORWICH CASTLE

NORFOLK

Norwich Castle occupies a lofty position overlooking the city centre, and it has always been a prominent city landmark. The Normans took over the centre of the existing Saxon town, and demolished 96 houses to clear a space for their castle. The first castle on the site, documented in 1075, was a timber motte and bailey castle. Later, in about 1130, it was rebuilt in stone to make it into a royal palace. The keep and the cathedral were built at about the same time, both of stone brought from

The ancient Norman Keep of Norwich Castle dominates the city below. Once a royal palace, the Castle is now the centrepiece of a museum housing one of England's finest regional collections of natural history, art and archeology.

Caen in Normandy, shipped across to Yarmouth and from there up the river to the two great building sites.

By 1096, Norwich had become so important that the bishopric of East Anglia was moved there from Thetford. Henry I spent Christmas at Norwich in 1121, and held the symbolic crown-wearing ceremony in the castle. The visit marked Norwich and its castle as the most important royal stronghold in East Anglia.

The gigantic square keep, 30m (100ft) across, resembles Falaise and is one of the few English keeps to have been built by Henry I. The keep has three levels. On the highest level is the Great Hall, with its Victorian balcony. The King's

Chamber was on a mezzanine floor and had a balcony, from which the King could look out over the heart of the city of Norwich. The middle level has a false floor which now houses the main museum display. The lowest level, newly opened to the public, has interactive museum displays.

There is a long stone Norman staircase leading up the east wall of the keep to a first-floor entrance in the Bigod Tower. This opens into a large northern chamber, which was the soldiers' hall. The southern half of this floor was subdivided into a knights' chamber, guard room and chapel. Diagonal partitions existed on the west to make a kitchen, pantry and constable's chamber. In the middle was the all-important well.

In 1340, Norwich Castle was handed over to the County Sheriff to become a common prison, and it became a place of confinement, interrogation, trial and execution. In the wake of the Dissolution, eleven unfortunate conspirators were executed for treason at Norwich Castle in 1537. Their fellow prisoners were interrogated to find out how far the conspiracy extended. The contemporary records tell us of 'Examinations takyn at Casthill of Norwich . . . before Sir Roger Towneshend and Sir John Jermy knyghts, Robert Holdryche and John Clere, esquires.' Prisoner after prisoner recalled scraps of conversation that meant nothing at all. One wonders if anybody, the eleven dead included, had committed any crime whatever.

In 1834–39, the exterior of Norwich Castle was refaced and the interior gutted. In 1894, the castle was turned into a museum. The recent face-lift to re-vamp the museum cost £11.8 million. It contains, among many other items of interest, the Snettisham Treasure, a gibbet and the death masks of many of the unfortunate people who were hanged at the Castle.

ORFORD CASTLE

SUFFOLK

Orford Castle is one of Henry II's castles, built at huge expense in the 1160s. The King spent £663 on Orford in the year 1166 alone. The castle stands close to the bleak, windswept coast of Suffolk, on the River Alde, with the intention of asserting the King's authority over East Anglia, and in particular challenging the power of Hugh Bigod, the Earl of Norfolk. It overlooks Orford, which was then a busy, thriving port.

For this building, Henry encouraged his designer to move away from the standard keep design – a cube with a tower at each corner – towards a circular plan by way of a polygon. The tower is a remarkable 21-sided tower. The inspiration for this innovative design seems to have come from the European mainland, though it is still unclear whether it came from Denmark, Sweden or France. In any event, his designer was well up to the challenge. In Maurice the Engineer, Henry II had found the ideal military architect for his purposes. Orford stands complete, a kind of freak, a clumsy prototype of the truly cylindrical keeps that would be built in England in the thirteenth century.

Orford Castle, its walls built of cheap local flint and expensively imported Caen stone from Normandy, was habitable by the year 1168. By 1170, the fateful year of Thomas Becket's assassination at Canterbury, the keep was fitted with an equally innovative curtain wall with rectangular towers. Unfortunately, the curtain wall has now gone. All we are left with is the astonishing polygonal keep built in 1165–67. It has squarish angle-towers, just as if the keep was a conventional cube shape, but they huddle round a rather compressed polygonal core – and there are three of them instead of the expected four. The circular interior contains many rooms distributed across five floors, including kitchens and a chapel. From the top of the tower, 27m up, there is a fine view across Orford Ness.

Towering polygonal keeps like Orford and Conisbrough turned out to be experimental and transitional. In succeeding decades, the well-tried traditional cube shaped keeps went on being built, and the polygonal keep evolved into a strong new type, the big round keep. But Orford Castle was an important step in the development of Henry II's ideas on castle-building. In the thirty-three years of Henry II's reign, about £21,000 was spent on castles. Of that sum, around two-thirds went on minor repairs and modifications – and of course maintenance. Most of the rest was spent on the building of just six castles – Dover, Newcastle, Nottingham, Winchester, Windsor and Orford. On each of these six castles he spent at least £1,000.

After King John's death, the castle was taken by the French claimant to the throne, Prince Louis. Orford was to change hands several times subsequently.

The fine stonework of Maurice the Engineer's castle remains virtually intact; it has not been involved in any military action, and that has saved it.

OXBURGH HALL

NORFOLK

It was in 1482 that Sir Edmund Bedingfield was granted his licence to crenellate Oxburgh by King Edward IV. Bedingfield built the moated manor house that he coveted as a fashionable status symbol. He could not afford a castle, but had sufficient funds and status to build a moated mansion that looked like a castle.

Since Sir Edmund's day there have been a few changes. One is the demolition of the Great Hall in 1775, and the house as a whole was extensively remodelled in the middle of the nineteenth century. At that time the house was lavishly enhanced inside with a suite of fake Tudor rooms; outside, some pretty little oriel windows, bay windows and fancy twisted chimneys made out of terracotta have given the building a distinctly Gothic appearance. The underlying structure is nevertheless still the late fifteenth century one.

Oxburgh Hall has been the home of the Bedingfield family since well before the present house was built, and there are still family members living there.

In the sixteenth and seventeenth centuries, the Bedingfields were repeatedly persecuted for their Catholicism, though they steadfastly remained loyal to the Crown. Henry VII visited Oxburgh Hall in 1487, and since then the room he slept in has naturally been called the King's Room. In the centre cabinet of this room are the written instructions from Henry VIII to Sir Edmund Bedingfield regarding the arrangements for the funeral of his ex-wife, Catherine of Aragon.

Elizabeth I visited Oxburgh Hall in 1578, which is surprising. As a princess during the reign of her half-sister, Elizabeth had been kept prisoner in the Tower of London in the custody of Sir Henry Bedingfield, and then under house arrest at Woodstock again in Sir Henry's custody. Surely she had had enough of Bedingfield's hospitality, or was it the Queen's idea of a joke?

Oxburgh contains many interesting features, including a fine parterre garden to the east and a walled Victorian kitchen garden. There is a wood called 'My Lady's Wood'. There is a magnificent spiral staircase made of brick, leading from the armoury up to the roof, from which there are magnificent views of the surrounding countryside. In a small room next to the King's Room are preserved the embroidered wall hangings made by Mary Queen of Scots during her captivity at Tutbury Castle. These 'Marian' hangings represent many hours of painstaking work by Mary and Elizabeth Countess of Shrewsbury (later 'Bess of Hardwick'), who

sewed with the Scottish Queen to keep her company.

Just outside the grounds of the Hall is the partly ruined parish church. Attached to it is a small chantry chapel, where members of the Bedingfield family were buried from the time of Sir Edmund until the late eighteenth century. The chantry has recently been restored, and has some beautiful early Renaissance terracotta screens.

Oxburgh Hall was once a high status residence, and that can still be appreciated thanks to the careful maintenance of the old building. Twentieth century restoration work included the manufacture of reproduction rolls of some of the spectacular wallpapers by using surviving scraps of the original wallpaper.

The first sight of the Hall, through the walled garden, presents a perfect medieval moated manor house, entered through a semi-fortified gatehouse. The mellow brickwork we still see today was an up and coming building material in the fifteenth century, and required great skill on the part of the brickmakers and builders as well as great wealth on the part of the owner.

TATTERSHALL CASTLE

LINCOLNSHIRE

In the fifteenth century, a new fashion developed, for what has been called 'bastard feudalism'. This new style consisted of the addition of very capacious towers, large enough for the feudal lord and his retainers to live in, embedded in the castle's curtain wall. Warwick Castle is a classic example of this. In effect, the central keep was dispensed with; its functions were instead incorporated into the curtain wall. The towers built at this time are easily identified as they are often made of red brick. The finest of them all is Tattershall Castle. Like Bodiam, Tattershall was rescued and restored back to its medieval state. Tattershall Castle's rescuer was Lord Curzon.

Henry VI's Treasurer, Lord Cromwell, became one of the richest men in England. It seems that much of his wealth was acquired dishonestly. In his will dated 1455 he left his executors the task of paying back, 'for conscience's sake', over £5,000 which he had extorted from various people. At Tattershall in Lincolnshire he built and endowed a magnificent church where he asked for perpetual prayers to be said for his soul. It stands next to the castle.

The huge tower, which still stands intact, was erected on the west side of the inner bailey of a thirteenth century castle. It is grotesquely oversized for the bailey, and looks very peculiar without the curtain wall. Nearly everything other than the tower has gone, but it is evident that the overall defence works were impressive.

There is a vaulted basement in the tower, and then four storeys above that, the whole structure standing 37m (120ft) high to the top of the turrets; it is almost as high as the Norman keep at Rochester. The three upper storeys were Cromwell's accommodation, each with a large hall and side chambers. There are wide spiral staircases, splendid fireplaces and traceried windows. The walls bear carved armorial bearings. It is clear that Cromwell lived here in great style, and it is easy to imagine the walls hung with expensive tapestries, the rooms fitted with grandiose furniture, and processions of liveried servants carrying trays of food and waiting at table.

It looks as if Cromwell built for show rather than security. There are battlements and a moat, it is true, but there are three entrances, all of them weakly defended. The tower also has large windows, which would have made it vulnerable to bombardment.

What Lord Cromwell built for himself at Tattershall was not so much a castle as a palace built to look like a castle – hence the term 'bastard feudalism'. Tattershall Castle was really a very grandiose version of the little moated manor houses that were springing up all over England, the homes of lords and even knights who wanted to live out the fantasy – already a nostalgic dream – of living in castles. The last of these medieval fakes was probably Thornbury in Gloucestershire, which was built by the Duke of Buckingham in 1511. Then the age of castles was really over – though it took the Civil War, and another Cromwell, to prove it.

The great red brick tower at Tattershall reaches a height of 30.5 metres (100 ft) and is a prominent feature in the local landscape. Records show that nearly one million locally-made bricks were used in the construction of the tower and associated buildings, which are considered to be some of the best examples of medieval brickwork in the country.

BELVOIR CASTLE

LEICESTERSHIRE

Belvoir Castle is now more a mansion than a true castle, a stately home rather than a fortress. It nevertheless began life as a true castle, an earth and timber fort raised in the years after the Norman Conquest. It was built by Robert de Todeni, who served as William the Conqueror's standard bearer at the Battle of Hastings. The simple motte castle (a keep on a mound) that stood on the site in the 1080s was typical of those being raised all over England at that time.

Not much is known of the initial fortification, but the early timber castle was replaced in stone. A medieval seal shows the castle with a big rectangular keep and a masonry curtain wall surrounding it.

The castle's name is Norman French and means 'beautiful view', but it has been in English usage for so many hundreds of years that it is pronounced 'Beaver'.

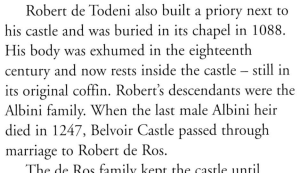

Belvoir Castle in Leicestershire must more accurately be viewed as a stately home. However, it did begin its life as a true castle, an earth and timber fortification erected in the years shortly after the Norman Conquest. Pronounced 'beaver', the castle's majestic name dates back to Norman times and means 'beautiful view', a very apt title for this picturesque estate.

Robert de Todeni also built a priory next to his castle and was buried in its chapel in 1088. His body was exhumed in the eighteenth century and now rests inside the castle – still in its original coffin. Robert's descendants were the Albini family. When the last male Albini heir died in 1247, Belvoir Castle passed through marriage to Robert de Ros.

The de Ros family kept the castle until 1464, when Thomas, Lord Ros, was executed for supporting the Lancastrians in the Wars of the Roses. After that, Belvoir Castle passed to William, Lord Hastings. Unfortunately, Belvoir was fated to fall into a ruinous state after an attack by friends of Lord Ros and quarrying by Lord Hastings, who used the roof lead and stone for another castle, Ashby de la Zouch. After Lord Hastings's disastrous asset-stripping, Belvoir Castle became a complete ruin.

After Henry VII seized the throne, Belvoir Castle was once again granted to the de Ros

family. Thomas Manners, first Earl of Rutland, instigated the castle's rebirth in 1523. His efforts at rebuilding were completed 32 years later by the second earl. What emerged was a typical Tudor mansion, a lightly fortified manor house. From that time on, Belvoir Castle has remained in the hands of the Rutlands, first earls and later dukes.

This Tudor Belvoir was fated to be destroyed as well, in the Civil War. Its Royalist garrison was besieged in 1645 and in 1649 Cromwell ordered its slighting. A new castle was raised on the site, starting in 1654 and finishing in 1668. Remarkably, the Belvoir Castle we see today is not even this Stuart castle but yet another rebuild! Much of the seventeenth century castle was torn down, and it was not rebuilt again until the nineteenth century. A fire devastated the structure in 1816, yet still the castle was revived.

In spite of all these destructions, Belvoir Castle is today one of the most magnificent stately homes in England, though in questionable taste. The exterior is a profusion of architectural shapes modelled in cream and orange stone, with windows, balconies, turrets, machicolations and battlements, with both square and round towers. The interior of Belvoir is equally sumptuous, with vaulting, arcading, brightly gilded ceilings and a large collection of statues, portraits and other paintings.

KENILWORTH CASTLE

LEICESTERSHIRE

The first stone castle at Kenilworth was probably the huge square keep built on the high ground that was earlier occupied by an earth and timber motte and bailey castle. It was a common pattern with English castles – an early Norman wooden fort, quickly raised to confirm and consolidate William's conquest of England, followed a few decades afterwards by a rebuild in stone.

Work on the stone keep probably began in 1174, when Henry II bought the castle from the Clinton family. Further buildings were added by King John and Henry III. It was Henry III who had the elaborate and original water defences installed; these became a major part of Kenilworth's security. Unfortunately they have now completely gone, but it is known that they involved the damming of several streams to make a very large artificial lake known as 'the Mere'. This extended for almost a mile to the west of the castle, and effectively defended it from the west and south. Further pools and moats were made to defend the castle's northern and eastern sides.

Henry III foolishly gave Kenilworth Castle to Simon de Montfort in 1253. Simon, Earl of Leicester, was the king's brother-in-law. By 1256, Simon had taken the leadership of the English barons who opposed the King's weakness and extravagance. Political opposition to the King quickly developed into military opposition, and de Montfort won a spectacular victory over the King at the Battle of Lewes in 1264, capturing both the King and his son, Prince Edward. This victory made Simon a virtual king, but his success was short-lived. Prince Edward managed to escape and gather an army against de Montfort, who was defeated and killed at Evesham in 1265.

De Montfort's son, also called Simon, held Kenilworth, but the following year Henry III and his son, the future Edward I, personally directed their troops in a siege of the castle. Kenilworth held out for several months, thanks mainly to the water defences. Prince Edward mounted an attack over the narrowest of the moats, using wooden siege-towers with catapults on top to hurl boulders at the defenders. He also had barges brought in from Chester, and used these to attack the castle by water – at night. In the end it was shortage of food and an outbreak of fever that made the garrison surrender.

Henry III then granted the castle to his own son, Edmund Earl of Lancaster. In 1361, Kenilworth passed by marriage into the hands of John of Gaunt, who built the opulent Great Hall over a vaulted undercroft on the west side of the keep. With these and ancillary buildings, John of Gaunt made Kenilworth comfortable as well as secure. It was now a palace as well as a castle.

In 1399, the castle became the property of John of Gaunt's son, Henry IV, remaining in the hands of the monarch for a century and a half. Then Elizabeth I bestowed

'The annals of this extensive and illustrious fortress are replete with interesting and curious facts, and embrace a great variety of incidents and events calculated to display the national customs and domestic arrangements of our puissant barons, from early epochs of Norman domination in England to the termination of Elizabeth's reign. In contemplating the bold fragments and shattered ruins of this castle, and reflecting on the scenes of warfare and rude pageantry which have prevailed here at different and distant ages, the mind is at once fully occupied and delighted.'

THE PENNY MAGAZINE
July 31, 1835

Kenilworth Castle on her favourite, Robert Dudley, shortly before she bestowed yet another favour, the Earldom of Leicester. Dudley spent a lot of money – £60,000 – altering the castle and laying out fine gardens with arbours and parterres. He entertained the Queen at the improved Kenilworth in lavish style for three weeks in 1575. It is said that Dudley's house-guest and her entourage, which included 31 barons and 400 servants, cost him a thousand pounds a day – and this was her third visit to Kenilworth. For his Queen's entertainment, Dudley laid on music, dancing, hunting and bear-baiting, prize-fighting, pageants, masques and fireworks, to say nothing of the banquets. The Queen loved it all. When she arrived, to the sound of trumpets, the clock on the keep, at that time fancifully named 'Caesar's Tower', was dramatically stopped to indicate that time itself stood still for the duration of the Queen's visit. To indicate her pleasure at Dudley's hospitality, and to show what a good mood she was in, she knighted Thomas Cecil, the eldest son of Lord Burghley, and four other gentlemen.

On 27 July 1575, the Queen rode majestically off to Chartley in Staffordshire, where she expected to be expensively entertained by another of her subjects, Lord Essex. She toured England, bankrupting her loyal subjects. That high summer royal visit was, even so, the high point in Kenilworth's history. When Robert Dudley, Earl of Leicester, died, Kenilworth passed through the hands of several noblemen until the time of the Civil War, when it would suffer the fate of many other English castles.

Cromwell's troops slighted Kenilworth's beautiful sandstone walls and towers, rooted up the magnificent gardens and drained the lake. The local Parliamentarian commander, Major Hawkesworth, converted Leicester's gatehouse into a house for himself. With the Restoration of the monarchy in 1660, the castle fell empty. It was now completely deserted and roofless.

Enough remains of the walls for Kenilworth's grandeur in its hey-day to be imagined. John of Gaunt's Great Hall, 27m (90ft) long, is still very impressive, and well worthy of the King of Castile. Its huge Gothic windows are still there, in the

height of fourteenth century fashion. So are the fireplaces where the great Duke and his third wife, Catherine Swynford, would have warmed themselves. Before the Parliamentarian vandals struck it was described as 'a large and stately hall, of twenty Paces in length, the Roofe whereof is all of Irish wood, neatly and handsomely fram'd. In it is five spacious Chimneys, answerable to soe great a Roome: we next view'd the Great Chamber for the Guard, the Chamber of Presence, the Privy Chamber, fretted above richly with Coats of Armes, and all adorn'd with fayre and rich Chimney Pieces of Alabaster, blacke Marble and of Joyners worke in curious carved wood.'

In the eighteenth and nineteenth centuries, Kenilworth was considered a great and picturesque Gothic ruin, completely overgrown. Nathaniel Hawthorne wrote, 'Without the ivy and the shrubbery, this huge Kenilworth would not be a pleasant object.' In the 1930s, work began on clearing the vegetation and debris so that visitors could once more see the third stateliest castle in England. Unfortunately, many of them want to make their own mark on Kenilworth, and the soft sandstone has proved very vulnerable to their scratched graffiti.

NEWARK CASTLE

NOTTINGHAMSHIRE

In the English Civil War, Oxford was the best defended royal city, and Newark was the next strongest royal city. This crossing-place on the River Trent where road and river routes converged was regarded as strategically important from the earliest times; the routes were in use in prehistory. Roman defences were built there, and these were replaced in about 900 by the 'New Work' which gave the town its name. These Saxon defences were raised against the Danes.

The Norman castle therefore had a succession of predecessors. Early in the twelfth century, Newark fell under the ownership of the bishops of Lincoln, and it was they who built the very fine stone castle that was described in 1138 by Henry of Huntingdon as 'magnificent and of very ornate construction'.

This ruin of a magnificent castle occupies a low yet commanding position on the river bank, directly overlooking the river, the bridge and the Great North Road. The Trent makes a natural moat along one side. During

Newark Castle is a magnificent twelfth century stone enclosure fortress but sadly only half of this single-ward, quadrangle castle now remains. On the river front are the impressive remains of a range of buildings between two corner towers, while the north side is dominated by a fine three storey Romanesque gatehouse.

the middle ages, Newark Castle was added to and modernized. By the time of the Civil War, it was one of the largest and most powerful castles in England.

Towards the end of 1642, the Royalist generals decided to garrison and fortify Newark Castle and make it the centre of a large fortified area that could be used as a supply centre and rallying point for Royalist armies. The Royalists needed to retain control of the point where the Great North Road crossed the Trent in order to keep communication open between Charles I's headquarters in Oxford and Newcastle where his arms convoys from the Netherlands landed. The defences included 'detached works', which were mini-castles in their own right; one called 'The Queen's Sconce' had elaborate bastions.

The Parliamentarians made three attempts to take Newark. In February 1643, Major General Ballard attacked with 6,000 men, but there was a fierce counter-attack and he broke away. A second Parliamentarian attack a year later was even less successful. Sir John Meldrum attacked with 2,000 horses, 5,000 foot soldiers and eleven cannon. Sir George Belasyse, the Royalist governor of Newark, succeeded in capturing a Parliamentary monster cannon; it was called 'Sweet Lips' after a famous prostitute of the day. Meldrum build a bridge of boats across the Trent, but found himself surrounded by Prince Rupert and his troops and was obliged to surrender.

The third siege, 1645–6, was by a joint English-Scots force of 16,000, commanded by General Poyntz. This time a great battering-fort called Edinburgh was used, as well as two bridges of boats. Eventually Newark was reduced to 'a miserable, stinking, infected town' and the Royalist defenders were forced to surrender. The siege of Newark was the last major action of the First Civil War; inevitably, Oxford too surrendered within a few weeks.

Since the seventeenth century, Newark Castle has stood in ruins and is now in a very poor state. It is nevertheless still very imposing and gives a striking impression of its former strength.

In 1887, the grounds of Newark Castle were landscaped and, more recently, summer digs have unearthed Saxon remains, including a cemetery, pottery fragments and animal bones, helping archaeologists and historians to learn more about Newark's origins.

WARWICK CASTLE

WARWICKSHIRE

Warwick Castle stands on an impressive site, a hill with a steep drop to a river. The site was chosen by William the Conqueror, according to Ordericus Vitalis, and a castle was built there in 1068. William was determined to subdue the northern Saxon lords, and to do this he needed to create a network of strongholds. Warwick had a high mound surmounted by a shell-keep, and fragments of this can still be seen. On the south side its bailey was defended by the river cliff and the River Avon. The other sides were defended by a wide, deep moat.

The Saxon King Alfred began the systematic refortification of England, but the bulk of the actual work was done by his successors in the early tenth century. Edward the Elder and Aethelflaed, the Lady of Mercia. It was Aethelflaed who built the fortified town of Warwick, and there may well have been a Saxon timber fort on the site of the stone castle we see today.

Warwick was a typical medieval castle, with ad hoc alterations going on virtually continuously. Warwick was always held by the monarch or a powerful subject, so it always had a high political and military profile. In the Barons' War, Simon de Montfort attacked and damaged the defences; the Beauchamp took the castle over shortly after this and remained its owners for two hundred years.

Warwick Castle was given an expensive face-lift at the end of the fourteenth century by the rich and powerful Beauchamp family. Incredibly lavish and spacious living quarters were built in a massive range against the curtain wall overlooking the river. Although there is a widespread assumption that medieval people were filthy and lived in filthy conditions, the castles often give contradictory evidence. At Warwick, there were washing sinks fitted with drains in the servants' quarters. Medieval manners placed great emphasis on keeping hands clean, largely because people picked their food up in their fingers. Piers Gaveston, the hated favourite of Edward II, had a fork which he used for eating pears, but this was regarded as over-fastidious and camp.

The 'bastard feudal' style was in fashion. At Warwick, the Beauchamps built two big corner towers in the curtain wall symmetrically on each side of the gatehouse. Each contained several storeys of well-appointed and well-lit chambers with fireplaces, garderobes and bedchambers fitted into the thickness of the walls. Caesar's Tower is a beautiful development of a round

The ghost of Sir Fulke Greville still haunts the tower were he resided at Warwick Castle and to this day the tower is known as The Ghost Tower. According to legend, his ghost appears from the portrait hanging over the fire place in the study and walks about the rooms in the tower.

tower, a three-lobed tower, which looks like three round towers coalescing, It stands an imposing 41m (133ft) high from the base of its massive plinth among the trees down near the river bank. Each of its storeys has stone vaulting except the top one, making the tower as a whole fireproof. The lowest storey was a prison. Since the big round tower was known in France as a 'donjon', such prisons became 'dungeons'. On the top were two tiers of ingeniously designed battlements. The second tier is like a second, slightly smaller, tower standing on top of the larger one. Guy's Tower is similar in size, but polygonal and lacking the dungeon. The placing of the two giant towers implies an eagerness to impress, and they had a lot more to do with social status than military necessity.

Warwick Castle became a major seat of power in the middle ages, especially when Richard Neville, Earl of Warwick, was its owner. It was this Warwick who played a major part in putting Edward IV on the throne, and so became 'Warwick the King-maker'.

The earldom changed hands several times until in 1604 James I presented it – and the now-dilapidated castle – to Sir Fulke Greville. Warwick Castle remained in the hands of the Greville family until 1978. According to the epitaph he chose for himself, Fulke Greville was 'Servant of Queen Elizabeth, Counsellor to King James, Friend to Sir Philip Sidney'. He was content to be in the background, a support to others. He was a poet and his writings, mostly unpublished in his lifetime, show him to be a shrewd observer and moralist. He probably first attended Elizabeth I's court in Sir Philip Sidney's company in 1575. He was friendly with the Earl of Essex, yet somehow escaped retribution when Essex was beheaded for treason in 1601. He continued in favour with both Elizabeth and her successor, James I. He became Chancellor of the Exchequer in 1614. In 1617, James I visited him at Warwick Castle. After James I died in 1625, Fulke Greville attended Charles I's court. In 1628 he was stabbed to death by his servant, Ralph Haywood, who was angry at what he considered the ungenerous legacy Sir Fulke left to him in his will.

Sir Fulke's ghost is said to haunt the Ghost Tower.

The castle was bought by the Tussaud's Group in 1978 and extensively restored. The state rooms have been enhanced with some imaginative and

The grounds of Warwick Castle were landscaped by Capability Brown and over the years the estate and residence were tranformed into a grand Stately Home. George IV, Queen Victoria, Prince Albert and Edward VII were all very familiar with Warwick Castle.

incredibly life-like waxworks, thanks to the long experience of the Tussaud's Studios. One shows an Edwardian soiree, with a bearded gentleman in evening dress playing the piano, accompanying a young lady singing. Another young lady lounges on a sofa, listening and taking tea. The state dining room dates from 1763, when it was commissioned by Francis Greville; kings and queens have been entertained here. The great hall is the largest room in the whole castle. With its carpets and fine furniture, it looks far more opulent and comfortable today than it would have looked in earlier days. Instead of carpets, there would have been rushes. The room would have been smoky and the atmosphere dark and strong-smelling. The castle chapel is a small but beautiful building, erected in the early 1600s; it is thought that an earlier chapel stood on the same spot.

Warwick has many of its rooms on show, including drawing rooms, bedrooms, music room, library, smoking room, dressing room. The building itself is an exciting and inspiring evocation of the medieval past, and there are many events and attractions that are of interest. Of all the castles in England, Warwick Castle is probably the most worthwhile, the one that most repays a visit by the ordinary tourist.

ALNWICK CASTLE

NORTHUMBERLAND

The market town of Alnwick (pronounced 'Ann-ick') is dominated by the magnificent castle built by successive generations of the Percy family, who were first Earls then Dukes of Northumberland. The first Norman owner of Alnwick is thought to have been Gilbert de Tesson, William the Conqueror's standard bearer at the Battle of Hastings, but it is not known whether he raised any kind of castle at Alnwick. Tesson was probably deprived of his lands because of his participation in a rebellion against William II in 1095. Yvo de Vescy became Alnwick's next owner, and it was he who erected the first elements in the castle that still survive. De Vescy died in 1134, and his castle was then described as 'very strongly fortified'. The Vescy line ended when William de Vescy was killed at the Battle of Bannockburn in 1314.

The Percy family was founded by William de Percy, who came to England with the Conqueror, who bestowed on him a huge estate extending across Lincolnshire and Yorkshire. The most famous of the Percys was Sir Henry Percy, known as 'Hotspur'. At fourteen he took part in the Siege of Berwick and fought fiercely against the Scots when they invaded in 1388. Hotspur was captured by the Scots, and £3,000 of his ransom was paid by Richard II. He was also in favour with Henry IV, who gave him the castle of Beaumaris. However, Hotspur was later insulted by Henry IV and quixotically switched his allegiance to the dead Richard II, who he declared was still alive; he was killed at the Battle of Shrewsbury in 1403.

The original Norman design of Alnwick Castle can still be made out. In 1069, when it was new, it consisted of two walled enclosures with the motte, or keep-mound, in between. The two enclosures survive as the Outer Bailey on the west and Middle Bailey on the east. The motte would in the eleventh century have carried a simple circular shell-keep, though this was later replaced with something much grander. The castle was developed in grander and grander style, partly because the Percys were constantly and incessantly at war with the Scots and therefore needed a strong fortress, and partly because of their high self-esteem.

When Henry de Percy acquired the castle and the barony in 1309, he rebuilt the original keep in a new style – seven semi-circular towers separated by very short stretches of wall and tightly clustered round a courtyard. He also added the outer gateway and curtain walling fitted with imposing round and square towers. In about 1350, an imposing gatehouse and towered barbican were added. The barbican, a pair of very fine Octagon Towers with battlements, bears a row of shields depicting the arms of the various families allied by marriage to Henry de Percy, the second Lord of Alnwick who raised the towers. Originally, there was a drawbridge in front of the Octagon Towers and a portcullis within; the groove for the portcullis is still visible.

Inside the arch and through a door to the right is a typical bottle dungeon. Beyond this door, the distinctive 'dog-tooth' mouldings of a very finely preserved early Norman arch can be seen. This was probably built by Eustace Fitzjohn in about 1150, and was left intact when Henry de Percy added the Octagon Towers in 1350.

The extraordinary keep seems to have far too many towers and is far too big for its low motte. The Octagon Towers that form its entrance have their feet firmly on the flat ground in front of the motte. The overall effect is of a toy castle, though that is certainly not the effect the original architects intended.

The main entrance to the castle is on the west, through an imposing structure comprising a gatehouse and barbican which looks every inch a castle in its own right. It is in fact one of the most perfect of its kind in England and it was built in the time of the fourth Earl, the son of Harry Hotspur, in about 1440. Above the door is the Percy shield. There are also full-sized stone defenders, manikins quirkily added in 1764 on top of the gatehouse battlements. They look more like drunken guests at a house-party than defenders; they are, for one thing, tottering precariously on the coping stones of the battlements rather than standing on the wall-walk where they should be. They are in fact eighteenth century versions of medieval manikins – a common enough ploy to fool enemy scouts into thinking the garrison was bigger than it really was.

There was once a moat, formed by the Bow Burn flowing along the south and east sides of the castle, but this was filled up in the sixteenth century. Inside, there is a huge open space 100m (330ft) across. This is the Outer Bailey, big enough to house an army.

Alnwick Castle is the second largest inhabited Castle in England, the first being Windsor Castle, and has been the home of the Percys, Earls and Dukes of Northumberland since 1309.

In 1750, Robert Adam was commissioned to renovate the castle after many years of neglect, and this work went on until 1766. By then, Alnwick had been restored and transformed into a magnificent ducal residence in the fashionable new 'Gothic' style. To make the castle more imposing, the fourth Duke added the great Prudhoe Tower in 1854.

Alnwick Castle stands on a low ridge of pasture dotted with trees, in a beautiful setting of what looks like natural, rolling English countryside. It is in fact a landscape designed by Capability Brown, complete with a lake at the foot of the grassy slope below the castle walls. The overall effect is stunningly beautiful and evocative of the middle ages – and the might of the Percy family. The interior of the restored castle was furnished in a palatial Italian Renaissance style. After the exterior of the keep, the Grand Staircase leading from the entrance hall up to the Guard Chamber is startlingly incongruous. It is airy, ornate, with a blend of Carrara marbles. The Guard Chamber is nothing like a guard chamber, but pure Robert Adam.

The beautiful Library in the Prudhoe Tower is in a similar style but warmed by red walls, red carpet and the gilded spines of 16,000 books arranged in two tiers; it has three book-lined alcoves with fireplaces, with a light gilded book balcony above. It is a spectacularly sumptuous room.

Alnwick is exceptional in every way. It is, moreover, still an aristocratic residence, and can claim to be the second largest inhabited castle in England. This classic English castle was used as a location for Hogwarts in the film *Harry Potter and the Philosopher's Stone*.

BAMBURGH CASTLE

NORTHUMBERLAND

Alnwick and Bamburgh Castles, together with Dunstanburgh, form a trio of big powerful castles that in the late middle ages controlled the whole of north-east England.

Bamburgh stands in a spectacular location, on an outcrop of indestructible dolerite projecting like a pier into the North Sea. The dolerite is part of the Great Whin Sill, which is the largest intrusion of igneous rock in Britain and also makes the foundation of several key military defences; it is the same 30m (100ft) thick slab of rock that makes the inland cliff followed by Hadrian's Wall.

The castle itself is made of red sandstone. It stands on the same site as a sixth century fort which was the main stronghold of the kingdom of Bernicia, though nothing of this remains. It was in AD 547 that King Ida landed at Flamborough Head to begin the conquest of a swathe of eastern Britain from the Humber to the Firth of Forth. Bamburgh was at the very heart of this early kingdom, yet the early fort seems to have been a very unimpressive affair. Bede described Bamburgh as fortified by a hedge and a timber palisade. A Norman fort was built and in 1095 William II built a wooden counter fort when he wanted to lay siege to the castle. Nothing much was achieved until Robert de Mowbray, who had escaped from the castle, was captured. William II threatened to gouge Robert's eyes out unless the castle was surrendered, so his wife Matilda agreed to a surrender.

During the eleventh century, Bamburgh was gradually evolving and by the reign of Henry III the castle had become an extensive and well-established complex covering 2 hectares (5 acres). The castle site is narrow, in effect confined to the spine of the Great Whin Sill, and entered through an outer gatehouse with two flanking towers and a strong barbican. This leads to a succession of walled enclosures or wards. The fine big keep is an almost perfect cube 20m (65ft) high. With its walls up to 3.7m (12ft) thick it dominates the site and guards the Inner Ward.

Being so close to Scotland, Bamburgh inevitably became involved in the Border Wars. It initially stood up to bombardment well, but as weapons technology improved Bamburgh became more vulnerable. In the Wars of the Roses in the fifteenth century, Bamburgh came under decisive attack. After the Battle of Hexham, the Lancastrians were left holding only the castles of Bamburgh, Dunstanburgh and Alnwick – the three greatest castles of the

Bamburgh Castle is one of the finest castles in England. It is perched on a basalt outcrop on the very edge of the North Sea at Bamburgh, Northumberland. It commands stunning views of the Farne Islands, Holy Island and landward to the Cheviot hills.

north-east. Warwick 'the Kingmaker' and Montague, now Earl of Northumberland, brought the massive siege-pieces of Edward IV to bear, and with these powerful new cannons set about crushing the last of the Lancastrian resistance in the north.

On 23 June, 1464, Alnwick Castle fell to Warwick. The next day Dunstanburgh too fell. Now only Bamburgh was left, and Sir Ralph Grey, who held Bamburgh, refused to surrender. He was exempted from the general pardon. Bamburgh was attacked with cannons by Warwick, and it was not long before chunks of masonry from the ramparts were blasted into the sea. Resistance quickly collapsed. It was the first time a battering ram was used effectively in England. The King's huge guns, called London and Newcastle (both made of iron) and Dijon (made of brass) made quick work of the walls of Bamburgh. Once they were breached, Warwick was soon inside the castle. Sir Ralph Grey was seriously wounded in this assault, but shown no mercy. He was dragged off to be accused before High Constable John Tiptoft, the Earl of Worcester, and executed (*see* Ely).

That June, in 1464, Bamburgh won the doubtful distinction of becoming the first English castle to have its walls breached by gunfire. This significant technological breakthrough spelt the beginning of the end for all English castles as purely military strongholds. From that point on, the survivors increasingly became stately homes for aristocrats. Many of course did not survive, but were left in ruins.

After this disaster, Bamburgh languished in a state of disrepair for 300 years. During the latter part of her reign, Elizabeth I decided to give the tumbledown castle and its lands to the Forster family. Claudius Forster was a Warden of the Middle March (the middle route across the border into Scotland) and this was his reward. Claudius lived in the keep, amongst the ruins of Bamburgh, until he was 101 years old. Eventually the Forster family became bankrupt and in the eighteenth century had to sell both the castle and its lands.

The Bishop of Durham, Lord Crewe, bought the once-royal castle, with a view to repairing it and making it useful to the community. A windmill was built at the north end of the castle. The corn, which was ground here, was distributed to the poor. The bishop also set up a system of signals between Bamburgh Castle and Holy Island to protect sailors along this dangerous coast. In storms, men patrolled the beach, looking for salvage. There are still massive iron chains at the castle, which were used with shire horses for hauling beached ships up onto the hard, beyond the reach of the savage sea.

Bamburgh was acquired in the 1890s by the armaments millionaire Lord Armstrong. He rebuilt it over-enthusiastically in what he saw as baronial style, completing it in 1903. One architectural expert has commented that it shows 'the acme of expenditure with a nadir of intelligent achievement'. Bamburgh remains in the hands of the Armstrong family.

Archaeologists have made some exciting discoveries at Bamburgh. In the 1970s, Dr Hope-Taylor found 'The Bamburgh Beast' a tiny golden image of a fabulous animal. 2.4m (8ft) down, Hope-Taylor found evidence of human settlement – fish bones and carbonized seeds of grain – that were very old indeed. They dated not only to the time before the arrival of the Anglo-Saxons, but before the Romans. More recently, in 1998, a Durham University team explored the interior of the castle with ultrasonic scanning equipment. The idea was to search for man-made structures concealed within the ground. They found traces of ancient fortifications from the iron age. Bamburgh Castle is turning out to have a very long history indeed.

BEESTON CASTLE

J ust to the south of Tarporley, Beeston Castle perches on the edge of a spectacular sandstone precipice like a predator, peering down at the Cheshire Plain, which lies spread out like a map, far below. It looks impregnable. Yet its spectacular location belies its history. In the long saga of its 800 year long story, Beeston Castle has been captured several times – and slighted twice over. It is not nearly as invincible as it looks.

The entrance to Beeston Castle is at the foot of the hill, and there is a climb past fragments of the masonry of the outer bailey. A modern footbridge across a deep ditch cut through solid bedrock replaces the medieval drawbridge, and this in turn gives access to the inner ward. The semicircular towers of the inner gatehouse lead on to the highest, innermost area of the castle, right on the brink of the precipice.

Not much is left there, but there are stumps of very thick walls in crudely worked sandstone that show that it must once have been a very strong fortress.

Beeston Castle was built in 1220 by Randulph de Blundeville, Earl of Chester. Unusually, Ralph de Blundeville never built a keep at Beeston, presumably because he believed that the site made it entirely unnecessary. Instead, he raised a long curtain wall to enclose the sloping outer bailey. If an enemy force climbed that far, it would then be confronted by the great ditch and the rocky inner defences. After heavy rain, even standing on these muddy slopes, let alone fighting in full armour, would be difficult enough. It may be that the easiest way to take Beeston Castle was to make a direct assault on the rocky cliff, and this may be why in the Civil War a Royalist officer took that route into the stronghold.

The thirteenth century ruin of Beeston Castle is located on a rocky summit 500ft above the Cheshire plain with views of the Pennines in the east and the Welsh mountains in the west.

The castle was already in ruins by the start of the sixteenth century. It had been the focus of a battle between King and barons in Simon de Montfort's time, and then again in the Wars of the Roses. After that it was rebuilt and strengthened, changing hands during the Civil War in the seventeenth century.

Beeston Castle was finally besieged in 1646 by Cromwell's army. Beeston's garrison held out for four months under the command of Colonel Ballard. Then the food supplies were exhausted and Ballard was forced to surrender. The Royalists were at least not short of water, which was drawn from a very deep well cut down through the sandstone within the castle. But they were desperately short of food, and in the end they were reduced to eating the castle cats.

Beeston Castle's design was very innovative. For the first time a castle's strength did not centre on its keep, as Beeston has none, but on its imposing wall towers and powerful gatehouses.

BOLTON CASTLE

NORTH YORKSHIRE

Many of the castles in northern England have fallen into ruins or disappeared altogether after being pillaged by the Scots or destroyed in the Civil War, their stone plundered by the locals for their cottages and field walls. Bolton Castle is unusual, just in having survived.

Work was officially begun on Bolton Castle in 1379 by Sir Richard le Scrope, who was granted a licence to crenellate his house by Richard II in that year. Sir Richard jumped the gun a little, as a surviving contract shows that the Kitchen Tower was built in the previous year. Most of the documents relating to the building work survive. The contractor was a mason called Johan Lewyn, who also worked on Raby, Warkworth and Lumley Castles.

Bolton was built, like Bodiam, at a time when castle design was evolving. The gentry wanted the security of living in a castle, but they also wanted a fine-looking house that would make an impressive show of wealth and prestige. The castle had become a status symbol. Bolton lacks some of the elaborate fortifications some other castles had, but it was defended nonetheless.

The gate-passage has a portcullis at each end, not only to prevent intruders entering, but to trap them. If they succeeded in reaching the square courtyard, the intruders were still seriously trapped. There are slots in the walls of the ground floor rooms, so that intruders could be shot down. The doors in the courtyard corners were cleverly protected by machicolations; boiling pitch could be poured down on anyone trying to force the doors below. There were several staircases leading up to the upper floors, but all narrow. These subtle and refined defensive features came at a price, and the overall cost of the castle was £12,000, a huge sum in the fourteenth century.

The Scropes' first connection with Bolton seems to have been in 1149, when Hugh le Scrope was a landholder in Wensleydale. The fortunes of the Scrope family rose after William le Scrope was knighted at the Battle of Falkirk in 1298.

Bolton Castle is a spectacular medieval fortress, situated in the heart of the beautiful Yorkshire Dales, on the boundary of the Yorkshire Dales National Park. Many of the castles in this part of the country are now in ruin or have disappeared altogether after being plundered by raiding Scots or destroyed during the Civil War, their stonework being robbed over the centuries by local villagers for their own buildings and stone walls. But Bolton Castle stands proud to this day, along with the memories of the great family of the Scropes of Wensleydale.

The Scropes were soldiers, lawyers and diplomats, and they amassed large estates in Yorkshire. Richard le Scrope, born in 1328, was a great soldier, fighting at Crécy and Neville's Cross in 1346, taking part in the siege of Calais with Edward III and the Black Prince in the same year. In 1350, he fought beside the King and the Black Prince at the Battle of Winchelsea, a sea battle against some Spanish treasure ships. In 1371 he was created Baron Scrope and in 1378, under Richard II, he was appointed chancellor. It was while he was chancellor that Scrope received his grant to crenellate Bolton. Shortly after this, rivals challenged Scrope's right to bear arms, which was a calculated humiliation. At a hearing in Westminster Hall, Scrope was supported by the leading figures of his age: John of Gaunt, Henry Bolingbroke, Harry Hotspur, Owen Glendower and Geoffrey Chaucer. Chaucer seems to have based his own Canterbury Knight on Richard le Scrope. The judgement went in Scrope's favour.

CASTLE KEEP

NEWCASTLE UPON TYNE

The Castle Keep at Newcastle was first a Norman timber fort. It was rebuilt in stone between 1168 and 1178, when it cost the substantial sum of £1,144. The main focus of the castle was a cube shaped keep with a square battlemented tower at each corner; there was also a curtain wall, with a gatehouse near the south-west corner of the keep.

The castle was added to in the thirteenth century, especially during the reign of King John (1207–1215), when an aisled hall was raised in the bailey. At the same time a barbican, known as the Black Gate, was added to the north gate between 1247 and 1250.

Following the completion of the town wall in the middle of the fourteenth century, the castle was stranded inside the new defences. After that, the castle became redundant in purely military terms. Because of that, few attempts were made to repair it and in 1589 it was described as 'old and in ruins'.

In 1618, James I leased the castle to Alexander Stephenson, who allowed houses to be built within its walls. At the time of the Civil War, it was briefly refortified, and it became the last stronghold of the Royalist defenders of the town when it was under siege in 1644.

The remains of the castle were restored in the nineteenth and twentieth centuries. The keep has been restored several times, most recently in the 1980s, when crumbling stonework was replaced and the interior cleaned. In spite of many interventions, the Castle Keep at Newcastle remains one of the best examples of its type in England.

The accommodation consisted of one large room on each floor, with additional chambers, garderobes, stairs and galleries contained within the thickness of the massive walls. For defensive reasons, the keep was entered on the second floor by an external stair. On the ground floor there is a chapel. The Queen's Chamber and Museum are on the first floor. The King's Chamber and Great Hall are on the second floor. There may once have been another storey above this, but now there is only the roof, which offers a spectacular panoramic view of the city of Newcastle and the adjacent bridges over the River Tyne, which the castle was originally built to defend.

The Black Gate is a remarkable structure. It is oval in plan with a central passage 11 feet wide running through it, flanked by guard rooms. The lower half is in its original medieval form. The upper half was rebuilt in the seventeenth century, using the original stone; this is in effect a house built on top of the barbican, which looks both absurd and ugly. In the nineteenth century the Black Gate was a slum, accommodating twelve families and a pub. The top floor and roof were rebuilt in the late nineteenth century when the building was occupied by the Society of Antiquaries. The name Black Gate refers not to the depravity of its architecture, but to the name of one of its tenants, a Mr Patrick Black.

The Castle stands on a steep-sided promontory overlooking the River Tyne. It is a readily defensible site which has been occupied for nearly 2,000 years. Flint flakes and a stone axe head found in archaeological excavations hint at prehistoric activity.

CONISBROUGH CASTLE

SOUTH YORKSHIRE

Conisbrough stands in a rolling landscape of natural hills and artificial mounds, looking like an old sailing ship on the high seas. It was built in 1180 by Hamelin Plantagenet, the illegitimate half-brother of Henry II. In 1164, Hamelin married Isabel, the Warenne heiress who had inherited the manor together with its early Norman timber-built castle. The first Earl of Surrey, who had fought beside Duke William at Hastings, built the wooden motte and bailey fort.

What Hamelin built at Conisbrough was the very latest in military architecture, something entirely new to England - a cylindrical keep within a small single bailey all built on top of the motte. The curtain wall is 2.1m (7ft) thick and 10.7m (35ft) high, with round wall-towers at the angles. The keep was also built 27m (90ft) high, a good deal higher than normal, with walls 4.6m (15ft) thick at the base. Because of its height, Hamelin added six enormous projecting buttress-towers, which run up the full height of the keep. The design is in effect an improved version of Orford Castle, and was the architectural wonder of its day.

The keep is attached to the curtain wall at its strongest point, with one side exposed to the field; this meant that, in the event of total disaster – a successful siege – the garrison stood some chance of escaping.

The keep is faced with pale limestone ashlars, all remarkably still in place, giving the structure a peculiarly modernistic look, not unlike the brutalist-minimalist architecture of the 1960s. This startling effect is exaggerated by the scarcity of windows; it must have been a desperately dark and oppressive building to live in, though the interior was doubtless whitewashed to maximize the light.

The keep's interior was, even so, built with comfort as well as security in mind, especially in the upper levels of its four storeys. It has the two earliest known hooded fireplaces in England. There is a wide staircase with shallow steps. There are water cisterns at the upper levels, so that the inhabitants did not have to go down to ground level to fetch water. There was also a pigeon loft, which

was part of the Norman postal network. The upper levels housed a chapel as well, partly accommodated within the thickness of the walls.

The inner bailey's curtain wall and the other buildings in the inner bailey were added later. The masonry of these lesser structures was not completed to the same standard, so the architecture of the castle as a whole was never conceived as an integrated aesthetic whole. The ragged and broken remains of the ancillary buildings contrast markedly with the light, smooth masonry of the keep. The impression given is that the keep is much newer, but appearances are deceptive here; the truth is that the keep was built first.

The keep and inner bailey were reached by way of a narrow zig-zag barbican connecting it to the outer bailey. The outer bailey now functions as a public park.

Conisbrough Castle stands between Doncaster and Rotherham, in an industrial landscape. The castle nevertheless attracted the eye of Sir Walter Scott, who was impressed by it when he passed it in a coach. He later researched the castle and used what he learned as background for his great romantic novel *Ivanhoe*.

DUNSTANBURGH CASTLE

Dunstanburgh, Alnwick and Bamburgh made the north-east of England secure. Unlike the other two, Dunstanburgh has been uninhabited for centuries. It stands in an incredibly strong position, on a natural dolerite headland jutting out into the sea. The site was so effectively defended by the sea that walls were actually unnecessary along much of its perimeter. It is still difficult to approach. There is a walk of a mile and a half across moorland leading down to a hostile sea and the castle in dramatic silhouette - a fine view made famous by Turner's painting.

Possibly there was an earlier fortress on the site, but it seems more likely that Thomas Earl of Lancaster was developing the site for the first time when he struck on the idea of building his fortress there after the great English disaster at the Battle of Bannockburn. A virgin site, Dunstanburgh is a striking contrast to Bamburgh, which had been occupied and possibly fortified in the late iron age, as well as in the sixth century AD.

Thomas Earl of Lancaster was the most powerful baron in England in the reign of Edward II. The Earl and the King were in constant conflict, particularly over the favouritism shown by the King to his lover, Piers Gaveston. It was Lancaster himself who was responsible for having Gaveston captured and executed at Warwick. In the turmoil that followed this assassination, the Scots seized the opportunity to invade northern England. This is what prompted Thomas Earl of Lancaster to begin work on the great fortress at Dunstanburgh. It covers 11 acres, which is huge – large enough to corral all the people and cattle of the area if an invading Scottish army should pass that way.

The architect of Dunstanburgh, a mason called Master Elias, had worked under the great military architect and constable of Harlech, Master James of St George. Following his master's model, Elias made much of his gatehouse (1313–25), which is large enough to contain the great hall and other state apartments, and built of the finest materials. The gatehouse had to be powerfully defensive – the entrance was always a weak point in a castle – but it also had to impress and intimidate. James and Elias intimidated through sheer size.

Dunstanburgh was built on a grand scale. It had to provide space and protection for the local people and their livestock; the thick curtain walls and the steep sea cliffs gave complete protection on two sides.

Dunstanburgh was modernized in 1380–84, when Thomas Earl of Lancaster's successor as head of the House of Lancaster, John of Gaunt, was Lieutenant of the Scots Marches. John of Gaunt added a second gatehouse, strengthened the castle and provided more accommodation.

In the Wars of the Roses, the Lancastrian stronghold was besieged by Yorkists and fell in 1464; it was very heavily damaged. In the Civil War, Dunstanburgh was able to play no part; it still stood in ruins from the Yorkist cannons. It is still in ruins now, caught in the frozen moment of its surrender five hundred years ago.

DURHAM CASTLE

TYNE & WEAR

Durham Castle was built on the orders of William the Conqueror in 1072, on his return from Scotland, and Waltheof, the Saxon Earl of Northumberland, was given the task of building it. Over the centuries it was continually rebuilt, but it is still dominated by its irregular octagonal keep with buttresses at the corners. What we see is not the original building, but one built in the fourteenth century by Bishop Thomas Hatfield, and then later substantially restored. The keep is set on a mound of sandstone, with its walls going right down to the solid bedrock. Through the middle ages it was, rather unusually, the bishops who maintained the castle; they treated it as their fortified residence.

Durham Castle turned out to be useless in a siege. When the Northern Earls rose on behalf of Mary Queen of Scots in 1569, they were able to take it without firing a single shot.

For many centuries the keep fell into disuse. It was eventually rebuilt in 1838–40 to accommodate students; this was when the castle became Durham University.

The older part of the castle surrounds the keep on its high motte. This triangular courtyard or bailey is entered by way of a gatehouse close to the site of the castle moat, which in turn was crossed by a drawbridge. The gatehouse was mainly the work of Bishop Pudsey in the twelfth century, but was modified in the sixteenth and eighteenth centuries.

The Great Hall was built in the thirteenth and fourteenth centuries by Bishops Anthony Bek and Thomas Hatfield. Beside the hall is a very fine octagonal kitchen with three huge fireplaces, built on the orders of Bishop Fox in about 1500. It was one of the great castle kitchens designed by the military architect John Lewyn. Only two have survived in England; one is at Durham and the other is at Raby. Within the Great Hall building is an impressive Dining Hall 30m (100ft) long

The older and greater part of the castle is situated around a courtyard to the west of the keep. The courtyard is entered from the gatehouse near to the site of the castle moat. The moat was crossed by means of a drawbridge just outside the gatehouse.

and 13.7m (45ft) high, comparing well with the huge dining halls at Christchurch College, Oxford, and Trinity College, Cambridge.

Palace Green separates the castle from Durham Cathedral, which stands imposingly at the southern end of the green. Up until the twelfth century, the time of Bishop Flambard, this area was the very centre of the city of Durham, with a market and a huddle of wooden houses. Flambard cleared them all because he considered them a fire hazard.

The buildings of the bailey, ranged along the edge of the cliff above the river, make one side of the triangle. Most of the houses in the North and South Bailey are Georgian, and they were very fashionable town houses in the eighteenth century. A famous resident in the nineteenth century was John Gully, a one-time pugilist, who in 1805 managed to last 50 rounds with the champion boxer Henry 'Game Chicken' Pearce before being defeated. Shortly afterwards, Gully became champion of all England by defeating 'The Lancashire Giant'. He died at the age of 80 after fathering 24 children.

Durham Castle has a fine setting, cheek by jowl with the town, palace and cathedral, on a high sandstone hill within a meander of the River Wear. Viewed together as a group, they make one of the finest architectural ensembles in Europe.

ETAL CASTLE

NORTHUMBERLAND

Etal Castle, at Cornhill-on-Tweed, started out as a medieval three-storey tower house. Unfortunately, it stood very close to the Scottish border, which rendered it liable to attack. In 1341, the owner, who was called Robert Manners, was granted a licence to fortify his house. What Manners then did was to create a square courtyard enclosed by a curtain wall, with the tower house in one corner and a substantial gatehouse in the corner diagonally opposite. The gatehouse was a big, solid structure with a portcullis, and it was originally defended by a barbican, joined to the gatehouse by a parapet walkway to the first floor. Between the two there would originally have been a ditch with a drawbridge over it. The two remaining corners of the enclosure were strengthened with towers.

The tower house itself was fitted with an additional storey and embellished with crenellations. Unusually, it had its own portcullis. The tower house is now only an empty shell. It had a meurtrière, or 'murder hole', under one of the windows. This is a vertical hole in the sill or floor of an oriel window allowing the occupants to drop missiles onto anyone attempting to break down the door beneath.

The overall effect must have been very impressive and powerful-looking. The curtain wall was nevertheless very thin by comparison with those of other castles, and it would have been very easy for any serious attacker to push through. The gatehouse was formidable, but no attacker would have bothered with it – given that a hole could so easily be made in the curtain wall.

The Manners family was engaged in a long-term feud with a neighbouring family, the Heron family of Ford Castle. This feud reached its climax in 1427, when it was claimed that John Manners, the heir to the Etal estate, had killed William Heron of Ford and one of his friends. Heron's widow complained to an arbitrating commission that her husband had been 'maliciously slain' by John Manners. In his defence, John Manners countered that William Heron had arrived at Etal with an army, leading 'a gret assault made in shotyng of arrows and strykyng with swerdes'. The judgement went against Manners, who was required to pay 200 marks to Heron's widow.

In the early sixteenth century, the Manners family moved away, leaving Etal Castle in the care of a constable. In 1513, Etal fell to the army of James IV of Scotland during his ill-fated invasion of England. The Scottish King was killed nearby during the Battle of Flodden, when his army of 30,000 was defeated by a hastily assembled Northern (English) Army.

In 1549, Etal Castle was ceded to the English Crown, possibly to ensure that it would be upgraded properly. The castle had fallen into neglect and the Manners family possibly were unable to afford to repair it. Etal was essential to the defence of the northern border.

The union of England and Scotland in 1603 changed everything. The Scottish border suddenly did not need to be defended at all. Etal Castle ceased to have any military value, and the neglect and decay accelerated.

Etal Castle started out as a three-storey tower house, but its location near the border with Scotland made it vulnerable to attack. Originally built in 1341, it was extended with a large gatehouse and curtain wall in the fifteenth century. The four storey tower became the keep and that is the part of the Castle that is still visible today.

FOUNTAINS ABBEY

NORTH YORKSHIRE

Fountains Abbey, which stands in beautiful wooded countryside three miles south-west of Ripon, is one of the three greatest ruins in England. It ranks with Stonehenge and Hadrian's Wall in international celebrity.

The early days of Fountains Abbey were architecturally unpromising, as it was a Cistercian house, and Cistercian monks preferred austerity and stark simplicity. The site too was a lonely and forbidding spot in the Skell valley, 'fit rather to be the lair of wild beasts than the home of human beings'. The abbey was founded in 1132 by Benedictine monks who were dissatisfied with St Mary's Abbey in York, where they believed that the rules of their order were not applied strictly enough. Bernard of Clairvaux, who was the champion of Cistercian reform, sent the breakaway monks encouraging letters and Archbishop Thurstan granted them land in Skelldale where the first modest timber shelters were built.

The new abbey took its name from a Latin description, Sancta Maria de Fontanis. All Cistercian foundations were dedicated to St Mary the Virgin, so it was 'Fontanis', 'of the springs', that became the identifying tag. The Skell too got its (Saxon) name from the springs rising on the valley sides nearby.

The stone building was begun in 1135, in Romanesque style, on a surprisingly grandiose scale and used the local sandstone. Its pale shades of pink, fawn, brown and grey are of the place and perfectly fit both the landscape and the architecture. The design followed the Cistercian rule – plain and unornamented, with thick round piers and round arches. There are also some pointed arches; it was the Cistercians who introduced this Gothic feature into England. The nave and transepts of the church were built first (1135–47), then the rebuilt domestic buildings (1147–79), then the rebuilt east end of the church (1220–47).

In 1147, at the climax of an unseemly row between the abbot and the Archbishop of York, much of Fountains Abbey was deliberately burnt down in a revenge attack by the Archbishop's knights. The building was gradually repaired. The rebuilding included a new east transept called the Chapel of the Nine Altars, which has incredibly high slender pillars, lancet windows and arcades on all sides. Even though now ruined, this chapel is still one of the architectural wonders of Europe. The octagonal piers have decorated capitals and originally had shafts of black spotted marble. All this is a long way from the original Cistercian conception of what the building should be. Evidently increasing wealth was having a softening and corrupting effect. By the Dissolution, any pretence at a strict Cistercian code had long gone.

Like other abbeys, Fountains was the economic hub of its locality. Its production and export of wool brought new prosperity to medieval Yorkshire, and helped the North to recover after William I's 'harrying of the North'. By the middle of the thirteenth century, Fountains was the richest Cistercian abbey in England, owning wool-producing estates throughout the huge county of Yorkshire.

One of the wonders of Fountains Abbey is the tall tower in Perpendicular style built by Abbot Huby in 1500–20. The Cistercians had always banned steeples and towers as extravagances and displays of vanity, but now Fountains had a splendid tower.

When Fountains Abbey was dissolved, its lead, glass and furnishings were taken by Henry VIII. The property passed through many hands and some of the buildings were demolished for stone to build the nearby mansion. But the depredations had not gone too far when, in 1768, Fountains passed into the ownership of William Aislaby, who lived at the nearby estate of Studley Royal Park. By this time, there was a 'Gothick' interest in noble ruins. Many landowners were building fake ruins. Aislaby acquired the real ruins of Fountains and developed the grounds around them to create a fine setting for them. What he created was a truly sublime romantic landscape. It was fortunate that Fountains Abbey fell into the hands of such an enlightened owner. It is thanks to William Aislaby that so much of Fountains Abbey is still standing today.

The nave is well preserved, a fine example of austere Cistercian architecture. It is eleven bays long and stands to its full original height; only the roof is missing. It is a great pity that funding cannot be found to re-roof Fountains, to ensure its future survival.

One of the finest features of the abbey is the undercroft or cellarium under the monks' dormitory. This runs for 91m (300ft) southwards from the western end of the church, along the side of the cloister and across to the river. It is almost as long as the abbey church itself, and divided down the centre by a columned arcade; nineteen columns sprout, unusually without capitals, into perfectly intact quadripartite stone vaulting. The arches at the church end are rounded. Those at the other end are pointed, showing that the structure was built

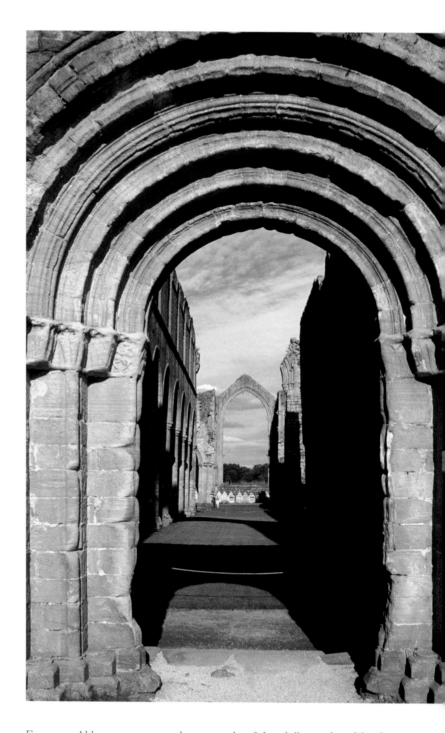

Fountains Abbey is an outstanding example of the skills employed by the twelfth century lay brethren, and is an unrivalled feat of medieval architecture in the United Kingdom.

across the boundary between the Romanesque and Early English styles. It may be that the Romanesque section survived the fire, and the southern section had to be rebuilt. The water supply and drainage system of the abbey were complex and their remains can still be seen.

In fact, many thousands do come to see the many wonders of Fountains Abbey. It is no longer 'remote from all the world', which is what the founding monks were looking for, but a magnet for tourists from all over the world. The best approach to Fountains Abbey is from the north-east, walking as William Aislaby did, from Studley Park, now a National Trust property, by the banks of the River Skell. From this direction, the visitor comes suddenly on an evocative and tantalizing distant view of the ruined abbey.

HELMSLEY CASTLE

YORKSHIRE

Helmsley Castle is an early thirteenth century fortress, apparently built by the de Roos family to guard the Rye valley, and to replace a still older castle that had stood on the same site in around 1100. The early castle is thought to have been built by the founder of Rievaulx Abbey, which stands nearby. Helmsley Castle was one of a group of medium-sized castles in Yorkshire, a group that included Pickering, Tickhill and Middleham, and all four of them were associated with hunting and the royal forests, even though they may have been in private hands. It is possible that they may have functioned as royal hunting lodges.

Although Helmsley Castle is badly ruined, it is still possible to get a good idea of its original layout. The inner bailey is rectangular in plan and enclosed by a curtain wall, which unfortunately has been almost completely destroyed. This inner bailey is guarded by an arrangement of round and semi-circular towers. The south barbican gave access to the inner bailey and was built as an outer gatehouse flanked by two round towers. From inside the bailey, you get a good view 'from behind' of the thirteenth century open-backed towers.

The south gate is badly ruined, but it is still possible to see the slot for the portcullis on the west side. To the north of the inner bailey, only the basements of the two gate towers have survived. Beyond that, the north barbican formed an outer gate; this too was flanked by round towers. Halfway along the east curtain wall stands the D-shaped east tower, which may have functioned as the castle's keep. It was first built in the twelfth century and later modified. The join between the older lower stonework and the later sandstone upper levels is visible. The curving wall of this tower has gone, but it is still possible to make out the internal layout of the building.

In the Civil War, Helmsley Castle was held by Royalist forces. It endured a three-month-long siege before it finally surrendered to a Parliamentarian army. As a result of this inconvenience to the Parliamentarian cause, Helmsley Castle was severely slighted after the siege. This was the common fate of Royalist-held castles in the mid-seventeenth century. The Tudor mansion built next to the west tower of the castle somehow survived this slighting more or less intact, which is remarkable, considering the carnage around it.

Part of the charm of Helmsley Castle is the fact that there are substantial traces of all of the various phases of the castle's history, from the early earthworks surrounding the inner bailey, and cut out of the solid rock, to the great Elizabethan remodelling of the west range and the systematic destruction of most of its walls after the Civil War siege. Helmsley is no longer the forbidding and threatening fortress it was in the middle ages, but a picturesque ruin. It is almost as if, in blowing it up, Oliver Cromwell was consciously preparing the way for the Gothic revival a century later.

Helmsley is an example of the transition in castle design between the older motte and bailey type and the newer fortification enclosed in concentric rings of stone defences. The only buildings still in good repair today are the west tower and the later mansion built by Edward Manners, the third Earl of Rutland who owned the site from 1563 to 1587. The castle only changed hands once in its history when it was bought by Sir Charles Duncombe in 1689.

There are three modern statues in the grounds of Helmsley Castle which were created by Malcolm Brocklesby in 1995. They are constructed of fibreglass to give the appearance of bronze, and the three figures are those of an Archer, a Pikeman and a Swordsman.

HEXHAM ABBEY

There has been a church on this site over for 1,300 years since Queen Etheldreda made a grant of lands to Wilfrid, Bishop of York c.674. Since the Dissolution of the monasteries in 1537 the Abbey has been the parish church of Hexham and today is still a centre for worship and witness to the Christian faith.

The abbey church at Hexham is bigger than some cathedrals. It stands at the highest point of the town, and once dominated both the town and the Tyne valley. The medieval religious house was founded in 1113 as a Benedictine monastery, so the 'abbey' church should perhaps more properly be called a priory church. Because most of the building works were done in the late twelfth and early thirteenth centuries, Hexham Abbey has been called 'the textbook of Early English architecture'.

Long before the Benedictine priory was founded, a church was built on the site in 674. The sainted Queen Etheldreda of Northumbria gave land to St Wilfrid, so that he could build a monumental church here. Most of the stone for this special building came from the Roman Wall camp of Corbridge. The foundations of the apse of St Wilfrid's church still survive. There are also some fragments of the nave and the entire crypt, which is one of the finest Saxon crypts in England.

A major point of interest in the crypt is the deliberate use of carved stone from Roman buildings. It is possible that in the last quarter of the seventh century Saxon builders wanted to include significant references to the old Roman civilization, which they saw themselves as re-creating. Other great Saxon buildings, such as Brixworth Church in Northamptonshire, similarly incorporated Roman carved stones, and Roman bricks too.

From 681 to 821, this great Saxon church was a cathedral with its own bishopric. In 876 it was sacked by the Danes. In 1114 an Augustinian priory was founded, lasting until the Dissolution in 1536. It was the Augustinian canons who built the existing choir and transepts. The transepts are unusually long, turning the church into an almost equal-armed cross. The south transept still has the canons' night-stair, which is very worn down by the feet of the medieval monks as they trooped down from their dormitory for services; it is still occasionally used by the abbey choir. The nave was destroyed by the Scots in 1296 and rebuilt as recently as 1908.

Hexham Abbey is richly furnished. Most churches lost their rood-screens at the time of the reformation. Hexham's survived. It was set up by Prior Smithson in about 1500, and has 16 painted panels of saints and bishops. In the choir, right above its presumed original position in the Saxon apse, is the stone bishop's chair known as St Wilfrid's Chair. It may have been used as a coronation throne for the Kings of Northumbria.

The choir has some fine fifteenth century misericords. The south transept has a big Roman gravestone commemorating a Roman standard bearer called Flavinus, and also the Acca Cross, dating from about 740; St Acca was a Saxon bishop of Hexham.

Although the church has been lovingly maintained, the priory buildings to the south lie mostly in ruins. The cloisters lay to the south of the nave and west of the south transept, with the refectory to the south of the cloisters. The monks' dormitory lay immediately to the south of the south transept. The west range included the cellarer's buildings.

LINDISFARNE CASTLE

Lindisfarne Castle is one of England's most recent castles, built in 1542. Beblowe Crag on Holy Island in Northumberland is a perfect site for a fortress, overlooking the harbour. It is perhaps odd that in its long history the island was never fortified before. Holy Island was given over entirely to the ecclesiastical activities of Lindisfarne Priory.

In 634, King Oswald of Northumbria gave the island to Aidan, a missionary from Iona. Aidan was made Bishop of Lindisfarne in 635.

Lindisfarne Priory was one of the great holy places of the middle ages. The Normans called it the Holy Island and it was they who built a Benedictine priory on the site of the older monastery, which had been destroyed by the Danes. It is the remains of the priory that can be seen there today. It is a fine piece of Romanesque architecture, still standing to a good height.

In that older, Anglo-Saxon, monastery the monk Eadfrith devoted himself to producing one of the greatest art works that England has ever produced, the 258 remarkable pages of illuminated manuscript known as the Lindisfarne Gospels. Before that, St Cuthbert was bishop here from 685, wearing his habit of undyed sheep's wool. He retired to the total solitude of Farne Island, where he died in 687. His body was returned to Lindisfarne for burial. Eadfrith 'at the first wrote this book [the Lindisfarne Gospels] for God and St Cuthbert and for all the saints in common that are in the island'. Eadfrith's remarkable book was finished in about 698.

The Anglo-Saxon Chronicle tells us that in 793 'terrible portents appeared in Northumbria . . . exceptional flashes of lightning . . . and after that the harrying of the heathen miserably destroyed God's church in Lindisfarne by raping and slaughter'. The Danes drove the monks out and they went, carrying the body of St Cuthbert with them. They eventually delivered it for burial in Durham Cathedral. Extraordinary tales were told of miracles connected with Cuthbert. Lindisfarne fishermen said that on stormy nights the spirit of St Cuthbert could be heard, between the rhythmic crashing of waves on the beach, forging beads for the faithful, using rocks as both hammer and anvil. The beads, they said, could be found on the beach after the storms subsided.

That was the old Lindisfarne, unimaginably holy Lindisfarne. Henry VIII changed all that. The Dissolution of the monasteries meant the end of the priory, which naturally became a quarry for the new castle. The priory church was turned into the garrison's main storehouse. Lindisfarne Castle was completed in 1550, three years after the wicked monarch's death.

The castle was never attacked. It was, however, briefly occupied by the French – for one night – and remained in a state of alert throughout the Napoleonic Wars. It was only after 1815 that its guns were removed.

At the end of the nineteenth century, Lindisfarne Castle was purchased by Edward Hudson, the editor of *Country Life*. Hudson then commissioned Edwin Lutyens to reconstruct it, which Lutyens did with great skill.

PRUDHOE CASTLE

NORTHUMBERLAND

Most of the visible masonry in this fine ruin dates from the twelfth century, though there was a still earlier Norman structure on the site. Prudhoe Castle has taken on many guises in its long history. It has been a great fortress, a baronial home and a major administrative centre. Its situation in the Tyne valley, not far from the Scottish border, meant that it inevitably got entangled in the recurring border wars between England and Scotland in the middle ages.

Prudhoe was at first owned by the D'Umfravilles, and only later passed into the hands of the Percys. The Percys were late arrivals in Northumberland. When William de Percy came over with the Conqueror, he settled at Spofforth in Yorkshire, where the family stayed for three hundred years before moving to Alnwick.

Prudhoe is laid out in a figure-of-eight shape. Curiously, its original inner and outer baileys are now separated by a Georgian manor house; this stands on the site of the medieval domestic buildings of the castle. Inside the inner bailey the D'Umfraville family built their great tower, which stands three storeys high, with added turrets. Of these, only the south turret still survives, but it gives an idea of the original appearance of the tower; the old roof line can also be seen, running along inside the west wall. The great tower at Prudhoe is its original keep. At Northam, the main building was turned into a ninety-foot tower keep in the fifteenth century, so Prudhoe is lucky to have hung onto its original keep, and it is thought that the Prudhoe tower may be the oldest keep in Northumberland. When the Percys took it over they found it unnecessary to enlarge it.

Right next to the great tower was a range of thirteenth century buildings, the 'forebuilding'. The eastern wall of this forebuilding was later incorporated into the eighteenth century manor house. Further west, still in the inner bailey are two round towers built in the thirteenth century. The one in the north-west corner of the bailey is still virtually intact.

The plan of Prudhoe Castle is roughly in the shape of a figure of eight.

In the outer ward the Great Hall was the most imposing of the early buildings, though not much more than its foundations can be seen today. East of the Great Hall are the remains of kitchens and other outbuildings, including a sixteenth century brewhouse.

The twelfth century gatehouse was a simple affair, a passage running beneath a series of arches. In the thirteenth century a Chapel was built over it. The Percys aggrandized the gatehouse, giving it the first oriel window in England, a fairly simple structure with two lancet windows, and then a barbican in front to strengthen it.

Prudhoe was still inhabited during the seventeenth century, but it had gradually fallen into neglect. In the eighteenth century it started to collapse. Early in the 1900s, the second Duke of Northumberland repaired and consolidated the walls that remained, but by then most of the ruins had been cleared. The castle is still owned today by the Duke of Northumberland, a direct descendant of Sir Henry Percy.

RICHMOND CASTLE

R ichmond is one of the luckiest of the great English castles. Somehow, it managed to escape entanglement in any of the destructive maelstroms of English history. Somehow, it remained in an untroubled backwater while other castles were besieged, bombarded, slighted, mined or demolished.

Richmond Castle was begun in 1071 by Alan the Red, who was the son of a powerful Breton aristocrat, the Count of PenthiÀvre. The fort was built to command the entrance to Swaledale. The keep Alan built was one of the very strongest the Normans built. It contains a larger volume of masonry in its fabric belonging to the first twenty years following the Conquest than any castle in England other than Colchester and the Tower of London.

The keep is a very imposing structure, a lofty double cube with four storeys, and the floor levels marked externally with discreet cornices where the walls step in a little at each successive level. The walls are pierced with a few very small round-arched windows; the interior must have been very dark indeed, lit only by flickering torches, candles and tapers. There are four commanding corner turrets and some fine battlements. The great hall is the oldest building of its kind in Britain, apart from Chepstow.

Richmond stands on a spectacular site, a high hill with a steep rocky drop to the rocky river bed. There are high moors on

The best preserved part of Richmond Castle is the Keep which towers over 100 feet above the town, and the walls are actually 11 feet thick. The Keep was a 12th century addition to the castle and was built over the original gatehouse (the archway at the base of the Keep is of the 11th century and is, possibly, the only remaining part of the original structure).

three sides, which made it very difficult for a big army with siege equipment to reach it. Richmond was virtually impregnable. The castle held a huge tract of the wild North under Henry II's control – with a vice-like grip.

Richmond's one claim to a place in history was its use as a prison for King William the Lion of Scotland in 1174. Other than that – nothing. There is no record of a siege or attack. History passed Richmond Castle by. This may mean that the castle was wrongly located. The military designer who sited it for Alan the Red, had he known his castle's future, would no doubt have argued that this was a measure of its success. A castle that nobody dared to attack or try to take had fulfilled its purpose effectively.

Given the unusual success of Richmond Castle, it is odd that it was allowed to fall into decay. This may be explained by its unprofitability. Medieval castles were expected to pay their own way. They did this by administering estates and dispensing justice. Being in a sparsely populated and poor area, Richmond made no money. By 1341, Richmond was reported to be in serious need of repair and also, ominously, 'worth nothing' in terms of annual income.

When John Leland saw it in 1540, he called it 'a mere ruine'. It says much about the strength of the original design and workmanship that, in spite of this incredibly long period as a ruin – getting on for 600 years – much of Richmond Castle is still standing. The magnificent keep is, astonishingly, in mint condition, just as it was when it was built over 900 years ago.

RIEVAULX ABBEY

NORTH YORKSHIRE

Rievaulx is one of the very finest ruins in England. Its soaring piers and arches spring from the green floor of Ryedale in such a perfectly picturesque way that it seems to have been designed as a Gothic folly by an eighteenth century landscape architect. It is hard to accept that, beautiful as it is, it was never intended to look like this.

When the Cistercian monks chose the location for their monastery, they described it as a 'horror and waste solitude'. But the austerity and difficulty of living there was part of the attraction. The cramped site forced an unusual orientation onto the church, which has its axis twisted by that of the valley; the altar is to the south-south-east, not the usual east. Even so, there is an irony in the extraordinary beauty of the architecture of Rievaulx. It was supposed to be a plain building. Abbot Bernard of Clairvaux wrote, 'What profit is there in these ridiculous monsters, in that marvellous and deformed comeliness and comely deformity? To what purpose are those unclean apes, those fierce lions, those monstrous centaurs, those half-men, those striped tigers? . . . We are more tempted to read in the marble than in our service books and to spend the whole day wondering at these things.'

Not long after St Bernard wrote this, in 1131, the lord of the manor of Helmsley, Walter l'Espec, granted land in the Rye valley to the abbot and twelve monks who became the nucleus of Rievaulx, the first large Cistercian establishment in

England. The Norman lord was a bearded warrior with a voice 'like the sound of a trumpet'. He entered the abbey as a novice himself, in his old age, then died there in silence after making his peace with God.

Within thirty years of Rievaulx's foundation, the third abbot, Ailred, presided over a spacious site occupied by a community of at least 140 monks and 500 lay brothers. They built their abbey out of the sandstone quarried nearby and at Bilsdale to the north, and they built it all in a very short time. The nave was built in 1135-40, before any surviving Cistercian nave in France. In early Cistercian churches the aisles were kept separate from the nave by stone walling inserted between the huge piers, but at Rievaulx these walls were taken out in the fourteenth century.

By then, the chancel (choir and presbytery) had been built, in a less than plain style with stone-ribbed vaulting and some Gothic ornament. The columns and arches were delicately fluted, which created a sense of extraordinary grace and delicacy, like pale silken drapery. The floor was decorated with glazed tiles in yellow and green patterns. This eastern extension to the abbey church, almost as long as the nave itself, was expensive, and it put the abbey heavily into debt. The chancel still stands

virtually complete, with its three tiers of arches and even the arch of the crossing still in place; only the roof is missing. It is an architectural wonder.

There was a huge cloister, 43m (140ft) square, which remains as a vast unenclosed lawn. To the east and south of the cloister lies a huge complex of monastic buildings, the warming house and frater, the day room, the novices' rooms, the treasury, the infirmary, the spacious abbot's lodging and the abbot's kitchen. The colossal scale of Rievaulx Abbey speaks vividly of the tremendous economic and cultural success of the monastic system – and of course of its unimaginable wealth. What organization today could afford to build on such a scale?

Rievaulx was isolated, but not isolated enough. Its location in the north of England made it vulnerable to attack by the Scots. It was also not sufficiently isolated to escape attack by the plague. By the time of the Dissolution in the mid-sixteenth century, there were only 22 monks left at Rievaulx Abbey. The property was granted to the Earl of Rutland. A village grew up near the site, built out of stone plundered from the neglected abbey buildings. It is fortunate, for us, that the abbey was not close to a large settlement, as much more of the valuable stone would have been carted off for re-use. As it is, the walls of the abbey still stand very tall in many places.

The chapter house, with its round apse, is an easy building to identify, even though none of the walls survive. It was built rectangular first, then the apse was added later. It was here, in the early years, that the abbots were buried. The gravestones of thirteenth and fourteenth century abbots can still be seen, together with the shrine of the very first abbot, who had been St Bernard's secretary and died in 1148.

The Dissolution took Rievaulx when it was already in decline. But when the abbey was in its hey-day it was not only wealthy but teeming with activity. The monks attended their services, summoned by bells, studied in

the library, tended their flocks of sheep, and warmed themselves on winter evenings in front of the two huge fires kept going in the warming house. It is easy to sit and muse among the ruins and re-create all this in the mind's eye. In the eighteenth century, the poet Cowper considered moving to Rievaulx in order to do just that all the time. Dorothy Wordsworth was equally taken with Rievaulx's beauty; she 'went down to look at the Ruins – thrushes were singing, cattle feeding among green grown hillocks about the Ruins . . . I could have stayed in this solemn quiet spot til evening without a thought of moving, but William [her brother, the poet] was waiting for me, so in a quarter of an hour I went away.'

These personal revelations followed Rousseau, and Burke's discovery of the sublime. By the time the Wordsworths visited Rievaulx, the Duncombes of Duncombe Park had built the spectacularly imaginative Rievaulx Terrace in the course of landscaping their grounds. They created a long, wide lawn perched at the top of the valley side to make a deliberately enhanced viewpoint from which we can still look down on the magnificent work of the twelfth century stonemasons in the picturesque valley floor below.

The spot was by a powerful stream called the Rye in a broad valley stretching on either side. The name of their little settlement and of the place where it lies was derived from the name of the stream and the valley, Rievaulx. High hills surround the valley, encircling it like a crown. These are clothed by trees of various sorts and maintain in pleasant retreats the privacy of the vale, providing for the monks a kind of second paradise of wooded delight.

WALTER DANIEL, *Life of Aelred*

SCARBOROUGH CASTLE

A Roman signal station stood on the headland at Scarborough. This was a tall stone tower 13m (43ft) square and 30m (100ft) high. On top was a semaphore signalling apparatus and a beacon-brazier.

The Normans were the next great stone castle builders. After the spectacular giant stone keep had been built at Rochester, Scarborough too got its own, smaller version, which was founded in 1135 by William le Gros, Earl of Albemarle. Like Rochester, Scarborough was thought to be impregnable. Henry II nevertheless proved otherwise. In a campaign to establish his authority, Henry smashed up as many as 500 castles. He was able to take timber castles relatively easily by knocking them down or setting fire to them, but he gained a reputation for storming even strong stone castles, and he did this by rushing them before the defenders could organize themselves.

Henry II first advised barons to relinquish royal castles in their possession. Some did, peaceably. Others hesitated. In 1154 the Earl of York hesitated, and the result was that the King stormed and took his castles at York and Scarborough without a fight. Scarborough Castle remained a royal possession until the reign of James I.

Scarborough was a large royal castle, and Henry II saw it as one of the keys to holding the North. There were medium-sized castles which, whether run by royal administrators or in the hands of friends, could be used for the routine administration of law and order. To ensure their security, he needed the power of the large royal castles as back-up; these included Scarborough, Pontefract, York, Richmond and Knaresborough Castles. Together, this powerful network of fortresses guaranteed him the command of the North of England.

King John was equally fanatical about castles, and he invested a large sum in repairing and reinforcing Scarborough, one of nine English castles in which he showed a special interest.

The only approach to the castle's headland site is from the west, and that is guarded by a strong barbican, a massive twin semi-circular-towered gateway with a flanking wall. The impressive curtain wall has eleven semi-circular flanking towers, and it is dominated by the tall ruins of a shattered thirteenth century keep. In the large outer bailey are scattered the remains of the Roman signal station, two chapels, and a medieval hall. Mosdale Hall was built by King John and rebuilt in 1756 as a barracks.

Scarborough Castle was besieged several times. In 1312, Edward II's much-detested lover Piers Gaveston took refuge there, and was starved into surrendering. In 1645, the castle was besieged by Parliamentarians, but they gave up and resumed their siege in 1648. George Fox, the founder of the Quakers was imprisoned there in 1665.

Scarborough Castle last saw military action, of a sort, in 1914, when it was shelled by two German battle cruisers. The damage done in the Civil War and the First World War has been compounded by damage done by wind, rain, frost, waves and time; the sea has gradually gnawed away at the castle from the east.

STOKESAY CASTLE

SHROPSHIRE

S tokesay Castle is one of the best-preserved fortified manor-houses in England. Late in its history, it was sub-let to farmers who used it for storage and neglected the fabric, but the walls are still in remarkably good condition. Seen from across the pond on the west side, Stokesay looks complete, but this is an illusion. It is mostly roofless and uninhabitable.

The location is remarkable. Stokesay now stands in a peaceful location in the hills of south Shropshire. But in the thirteenth century, which is when Stokesay was built, it was a very dangerous landscape, the Welsh border country, where Marcher lords and their soldiers slept with their swords. Stokesay, meanwhile, had a little moat, which would have been useless against a concerted attack.

The north tower of this toy castle was built in about 1240 by the de Say family. They built their house in a hamlet called South Stoke, which later added the family's name and became Stoke-de-Say. The de Says' choice of location seems to have been an act of faith. They rebuilt the adjacent church.

Laurence de Ludlow, a wealthy wool merchant, bought Stokesay and obtained a licence to crenellate in 1291, from Edward I. It is still not clear whether this was a genuine attempt to turn the manor house into a castle, or a bid for social status. Laurence de Ludlow's family lived at Stokesay for 300 years.

The manor house is built of green-yellow sandstone quarried locally. With its solid-looking tower and crenellated wall, Stokesay looks like a fairy-tale castle from the south, especially with its half-timbered overhanging storey added to the north tower during Laurence's rebuilding. The south tower has walls over 2m (6ft) thick, with garderobes built into them; these, as was usual in the middle ages, emptied into the moat. A well near the south tower is 15m (50ft) deep.

The two towers are connected by a banqueting hall, with unusually large pointed windows. The hall was originally aisled, with timber posts. At the southern end of the hall there was a solar accessible by an outside staircase, which was originally roofed, though now open. The solar has two squints, so that ladies in the solar could discreetly observe the goings-on in the hall below.

Built in the thirteenth century by a local wool merchant Stokesay Castle is technically described as a 'Fortified Manor' house, which was designed more as a domestic residence than for military defence. Perhaps the best example of its type in England - the house is remarkably well preserved and is now under the guardianship of English Heritage.

Many of the original outbuildings have now gone. There was, for instance, a kitchen block, marked now only by its foundations.

Across the courtyard there is a rather incongruous gatehouse, which was added in the sixteenth century.

Stokesay was clearly never intended to stand up to an organized attack. Cromwell's men laid siege to Stokesay in 1645. The inhabitants wisely surrendered immediately, which meant that minimal damage was done. Only the curtain wall was demolished. This originally rose 9m (30ft) above the moat and was decorated with battlemented parapets; a section remains near the north tower. We must be grateful for the cowardice of the owners; if they had not surrendered quickly, Cromwell's men would probably have pulled down the rest of Stokesay as well.

The Allcroft family, who bought Stokesay in 1896, have taken enormous care to restore and conserve what has survived of one of England's most important domestic ruins.

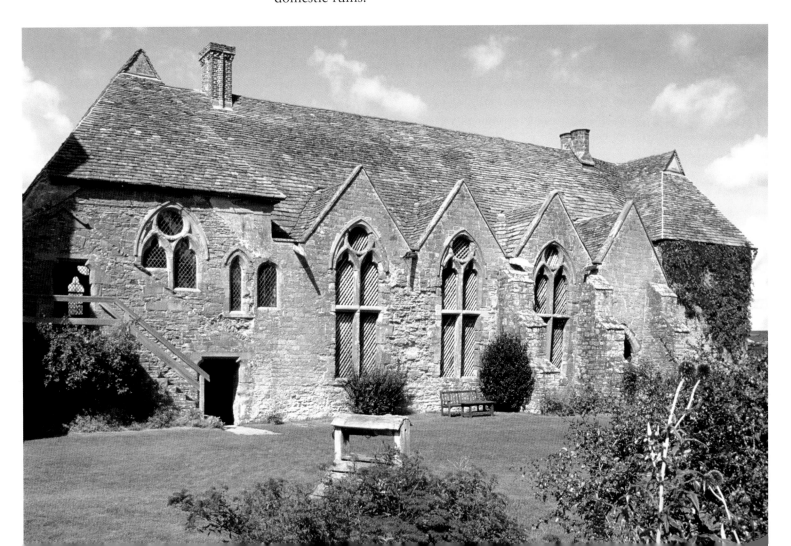

TYNEMOUTH CASTLE & PRIORY

TYNE & WEAR

The story of Tynemouth Castle is closely interwoven with that of Tynemouth Priory, which stands on the same rocky headland. The site may have been occupied during the Roman occupation, and there is also a local tradition that it was used as a military base by the Vikings when they invaded Northern England. Unfortunately, there is little to substantiate these claims.

Tynemouth Castle enters documented history for the first time in 1095, when we know that William II, William Rufus, succeeded in capturing 'Earl Robert's castle which is at the mouth of the River Tyne'. Bamburgh was taken at the same time. Earl Robert was Earl Robert de Mowbray, and his castle at this time probably consisted of an earthen rampart surmounted by a wooden palisade. Only later would the castle have been turned into stone.

When the nearby Priory was disbanded in 1538, the lands attached to it were granted by Henry VIII to Sir Thomas Hilton of Hilton. Tynemouth Castle nevertheless remained in the hands of the king. In 1545, a thousand workmen were busy fortifying the headland. Once the work was finished, a garrison of Spanish mercenaries was posted in the castle, and it became known as the Spanish Battery.

The castle played an important part in the Civil War, but then fell into disrepair. By 1681, it had fallen into a ruinous state and the defence of the strategically important mouth of the Tyne was taken over by another castle, the newly built Clifford's Fort at North Shields.

In 1900, Tynemouth Castle was a barracks and it had had many ancillary buildings added to it. In 1936, after the castle was gutted by fire, it was taken over by the Ministry of Works, who removed many of the additions and restored parts of the castle to something closer to their original form.

The great military strength of Tynemouth Castle really lay in the strength of its gatehouse. This is true of other castles too, such as Dunstanburgh, Bothal and Bywell. The gatehouse at Tynemouth consists of a rectangular tower with a projecting barbican – like Prudhoe and Alnwick. People entered by way of the barbican, along a vaulted passage protected by a portcullis and a gate, flanked by two towers. The basements of the towers functioned as guard rooms.

The open court beyond the Gatehouse was originally a drawbridge pit (a dry moat) which separated the barbican from the gatehouse.

The Gatehouse's first floor housed a magnificent Great Hall. This had a wide fireplace and was lit on all sides by windows. Next door is the kitchen with a wide fireplace and large oven. On the floor above the Great Hall is the Great Chamber.

At one time, the whole of the headland was enclosed by a curtain wall with towers. The western limb of this curtain is now mainly Elizabethan in date, but a fragment of the medieval Whitley Tower has survived. South of the Gatehouse stood two towers, though these are now only earthworks revetted in stone for artillery. Much of the south wall was destroyed in 1851, though one of the medieval towers was left standing. The curtain walls on the north and east sides of the castle have collapsed into the sea.

The priory ruins are approached through a massive gate tower set in a fortified wall. Yet these really are the ruins of a religious foundation. For hundreds of years the ecclesiastical function paralleled a military function The lofty headland guarding the northern entrance to the Tyne estuary must always have had a supervisory role. Even now there is a large coastguard station right next to the church.

A monastery had certainly been founded here by the middle of the seventh century. In 651, it is known from documentary evidence that Oswin, King of Deira, was murdered by his rival Oswy, King of Bernicia, and that he was buried at the Tynemouth monastery. Bernicia and Deira were the two ancient kingdoms of Northumbria. Miracles happened at Oswin's shrine. Oswin was declared a saint and the monastery became a centre for pilgrimage.

In the ninth century, its prominent location on the North Sea coast made it a natural target for Viking raids; it was attacked several times, in spite of its fortifications. The monastery was abandoned in 1008, and refounded in about 1090 as a priory of Benedictine monks; the refounding patron was Robert de Mowbray, the Earl of Northumberland.

Tynemouth's treasured relics of St Oswin were joined in 1127 by the earthly remains of Henry of Coquet a local hermit-saint. Henry died of self-neglect, a kind of church-sanctioned suicide, in a cell on the small island of Coquet, which lies off the coast near Alnwick.

The priory was once one of the richest in all England, with a presbyter 22m (72ft) high, whose soaring arches still impress. At the east end of the church you can see the Percy Chantry with its wonderful interlaced rib-vault design.

The monastic remains date mainly from 1090 to 1300, with the gatehouse added about a hundred years later. After the Dissolution of the priory in 1539, Tynemouth continued to be used as a castle, and the fortifications were added to in the sixteenth and eighteenth centuries.

Parts of the nave walls and the south transept of the Norman priory church are visible. At the end of the twelfth century, the apse at the eastern end of the Norman church with its three radial chapels was taken down and the church was lengthened eastwards to create a presbytery in Early English style. Substantial chunks of walling from this structure survive, almost to their full height. It is easy to get an idea what the church would have been like when complete by looking at its fine, though ruined, west front, which dates from 1220–50 and still has its west doorway.

A peculiarity of the priory church is that a large chamber was built in the fourteenth century above the ceiling of the presbytery and choir. It is not known what this unique room was for. A small door in the middle of the east wall leads to the fifteenth century Percy chantry. Its richly vaulted ceiling has 33 carved stone bosses crammed into it.

To the south of the church was the complex of ancillary buildings that were raised at every monastery and abbey. The cloister lay as usual to the south of the church nave, and the chapter house to the south of the south transept. To the south-west of the cloister and chapter house were yet more monastic buildings, including the dorter, the prior's hall and chapel, and the infirmary.

WARKWORTH CASTLE

Warkworth Castle stands on rising ground in a loop of the River Coquet, dominating the village of Warkworth from the top of the main street. The original Norman motte and bailey castle was built in the twelfth century by Henry, Earl of Northumberland, who was also the son of David, King of Scots. In 1157, Henry II succeeded in retrieving Northumberland from the hands of the Scots and in 1158 he gave Warkworth to Roger FitzRichard.

In the thirteenth century a new castle was begun with the construction of a gatehouse. It is located at the centre of the south curtain wall. It has survived with its archway and semi-octagonal projections on each side, though it does not stand to its full height.

In 1332, the castle passed into the hands of the Percy family, with whom it has always been most strongly associated. The Percys were the most powerful family in Northern England. They owned nearby Alnwick, which they treated as their fortress; but they regarded Warkworth as their peacetime residence.

The Percys made many major improvements to the old Norman structure. The most notable of these was the building of the spectacular great keep, which they built, all in one go, in the late fourteenth century. It is reckoned to be one of the very finest keeps in England, with an advanced design that provided very comfortable accommodation as well as major status. The keep is polygonal, three storeys high, and it looks impressive from any angle. Very unusually, the outer bailey was created over the site of the first castle.

Within the outer bailey, various wall footings show the locations and shapes of the buildings of the original castle, including a chapel near the gatehouse, a solar, and a hall running along the west curtain wall. The richly decorated Lion Tower provided an entrance to the hall and to the collegiate church, which was never completed.

The Percy family continually threw themselves into

The castle now contains one of the best privately owned art collections in Britain, focussing on Renaissance art and including works by Titian, Van Dyke and Canaletto, as well an exquisite collection of Meissen China.

dangerous conflict with the English monarchy and the castle was returned to royal control on several occasions. Their influence was so great, though, that a family member was generally reinstated before long. Harry Hotspur and the third Earl, his father, plotted to put Henry IV on the English throne. Three scenes of Shakespeare's play *Henry IV Part I* are set at Warkworth Castle.

The sixth Percy Earl died in 1537, leaving Warkworth Castle and all his possessions to Henry VIII. Later attempts to put a Percy back at Warkworth caused problems. The catholic Percy family came into conflict with the protestant Elizabeth I, recklessly supporting the lost cause of Mary Queen of Scots. A rising of the Northern Earls against Elizabeth I led to the execution of the seventh Earl in 1572. Warkworth Castle was pillaged by servants of Elizabeth I. After that disaster, Warkworth never recovered and it slid into decay and ruin.

The Duke of Northumberland still owns the ruins of Warkworth Castle, though they are maintained by English Heritage.

WHITBY ABBEY

North Yorkshire

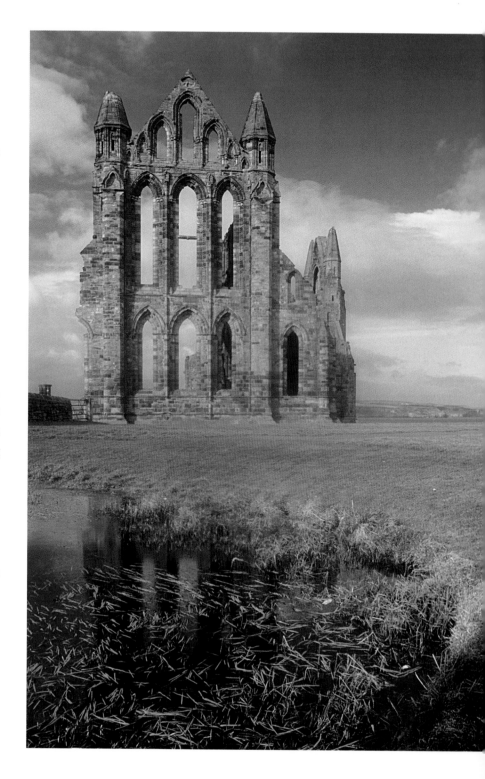

Whitby Abbey stands on one of the most spectacular sites ever chosen for a great church, a high, windswept headland on an exposed coastline. The abbey was founded as a monastery in 657 by King Oswy of Northumbria, to celebrate his victory over the formidable old King Penda of Mercia. The Venerable Bede referred to this community of both monks and nuns at Whitby as 'Streonaeshalch'.

It was in the year 664 that Whitby won a lasting place in English church history – as the venue for the Synod of Whitby. This was the great church conference at which the method for calculating the date for Easter (which is still used) and other matters were decided. Until that time the Roman church and the Celtic church were locked in a power struggle in Britain, and the Synod decided in favour of Rome.

The first major English poet, Caedmon, was a monk at Whitby. He wrote the hymn, 'Praise we now Heaven's keeper'. According to Bede he was an illiterate herdsman who in advancing years received a call in a dream to sing of the Creation. He then became a monk at the abbey under the supervision of St Hilda. There he turned biblical themes into Anglo-Saxon poetry. St Hilda, the Abbess of Whitby, was the daughter of a nephew of St Edwin of Northumbria. She was baptized at the age of thirteen by Paulinus and became abbess of Hartlepool in 649. She became the first Abbess of Whitby on its foundation in 657, and remained there for 22 years.

The monastery was destroyed by the Danes in 867 and it was abandoned for over 200 years. Then it was refounded as a Benedictine abbey by William de Percy. The abbey was finally dissolved in 1539. Although the domestic buildings were demolished at that time, the church was allowed to stand, probably because it was an important seamark. On its windswept headland, it was a major navigation aid. Unfortunately the abbey church was not maintained, and in the eighteenth and nineteenth centuries much of it fell down. In one of a shameful series of attacks on east coast towns in the First World War, Whitby Abbey was shelled by German warships.

Even so, enough has survived of the fabric of the abbey church to show what a splendid building it was. The chancel and north transept are still mainly intact, in Early English style. The east wall is especially striking, with three rows of windows with three lancets in each. For some reason that no-one has been able to explain, the nave is seriously out of alignment with the chancel. Very little remains of the nave, though the surviving masonry dates from the fourteenth century, apart from the west end, where the windows change to Decorated style and must be a little later. The cloister and the monastic buildings which lay to the south have disappeared. Remains of the buildings of the seventh century monastery have, unusually, been found by archaeologists. They lie to the north of the abbey church, but are not exposed for visitors to see.

Perched dramatically on the cliff top, Whitby Abbey is a magnificent reminder of the early church's power and dedication. It contained the shrine to the abbey's founder, St Hilda who died in AD 680 and symbolised the continuing Christian tradition in the north. The abbey's gaunt and moving remains have associations as diverse as Victorian jewellery, whaling and Count Dracula. There is a legend of a young nun who was walled up alive in the Abbey for breaking her vows of chastity.

INDEX